T0122015

WILL ROGERS
Views the News

Humorist Ponders Current Events

Robert V. Waldrop

abbott press®
A DIVISION OF WRITER'S DIGEST

Will Rogers Views the News
Humorist ponders current events

ISBN: 978-1-4582-0521-6 (sc)
ISBN: 978-1-4582-0522-3 (e)

Library of Congress Control Number: 2012913888

Abbott Press books may be ordered through booksellers or by contacting:

Abbott Press
1663 Liberty Drive
Bloomington, IN 47403
www.abbottpress.com
Phone: 1-866-697-5310

Cover photo of Will Rogers courtesy of Will Rogers Memorial Museums in Claremore and Oologah, Okla., Steven K. Gragert, director, and Jennifer Holt, curator.

Also written by
Robert V. Waldrop:

President Who Did What?

A fast-moving and entertaining look at all 44 U.S. presidents to date, how they got there, and what they did (and didn't do)

I Get the Drizzlies When It Rains

Here you can find an inside look at newspaper people, what they do and how they do it; it's really one of those memoir things, but with a focus on some remarkable people in the military, TV news and other activities

Contents

Dedication

My first thought was to dedicate this book to all those who know and love Will Rogers and how he looked at the world, and the people and events in it. Okay, I still do. But I also dedicate this book to my loving wife, Mary, and to our children, Michael, Bryan and Jill – all of whom have been very important in our lives, and who have greatly blessed me with their own humor and understanding.

Acknowledgement

My deepest gratitude goes to the Will Rogers Memorial Museums in Claremore and Oologah, Okla., and to their competent and friendly staff. In particular, I would like to thank Steve Gragert, museum director, and Jennifer Holt, museum curator, for their assistance. Invaluable resources were made available to me by them, especially through their *Will Rogers' DAILY TELEGRAMS*, edited by James M. Smallwood and Steven K. Gragert, published by the Oklahoma State University Press, Stillwater, Okla., in 1978-79. The *Telegrams* were further revised and reprinted online at www.willrogers.com by the Will Rogers Memorial Museums in Claremore in 2008. In addition, the Museums provide considerable helpful materials concerning Will Rogers on its website, www.willrogers.com, including a special section "Will Says," from which the writings of that name in this book were acquired. Additional writings by Will Rogers can be found under the heading of "Writings of Will Rogers" on the same website. Other materials are available by contacting the Museums directly. Many people have quoted Will Rogers over the years, often somewhat incorrectly, but the materials offers by the Will Rogers Memorial Museums are the genuine Will Rogers. Dates cited for quoted DAILY TELEGRAMS are the dates the TELEGRAMS were written by Will Rogers. It should be noted that Will Rogers did not always follow rules of grammar and capitalization in his writings.

Introduction

Will Rogers, who enjoyed an astonishing career being "just an ol' Oklahoma country boy," was somewhat more complicated than that. He was a devout American patriot. He made fun of presidents and kings, congressmen and movie stars, bankers and bandits. But he never did it in a nasty way, a refreshing alternative to some of today's comedians.

He even made fun of his beloved native land, which at first was part of the Indian Territory and later became Oklahoma, but he was always a promoter of the United States.

Much of the published fun he had with prominent people of his day – mostly in the 1920s and early 1930s – is just as fresh and to the point as it was when he first unleashed his barbs. And that is really the backbone, the purpose, of this book. This is not just another biography of one of America's greatest humorists; it is an effort to bring some people of today down to earth through Will Rogers's uncanny ability to let the air out of pompous balloons.

Will was a cowboy, a stage entertainer (rope tricks at first), then a vaudeville star and finally a movie star in both silent films and later in talkies. He also was a world traveler, welcomed in palaces and capitals everywhere. He also became a prolific writer, totaling literally millions of words in daily newspaper briefs and many articles.

His first newspaper articles appeared weekly through the McNaught Newspaper Syndicate. Then his daily "Telegrams" appeared first in the *New York Times*, and before long became Page One features in newspapers throughout the United States. He took whimsical looks at whatever was going on at the moment – one of his biggest assets was that his telegrams were available the same day to all those newspapers, rather than appearing days later as other columnists often had to do.

He never took anything or anyone too seriously – including himself. Often when he couldn't settle on some target, he would find something about himself to laugh about. He was famous for many things, including his own trademark comment, "I never met a man I didn't like."

He never let anyone forget he was part Cherokee Indian, and a proud native of Oklahoma. The small city of Claremore forever was his "city of cities." But he was not just an Oklahoman or part Indian – he was a citizen of the world, claimed and acclaimed by peoples and nations everywhere.

He tried to appear as just that ol' Oklahoma country boy, with an "aw, shucks" attitude, a drawl and very little education. Don't believe it. He had a shrewd insight into virtually everything, and many of his articles show his keen interpretation of some weighty matters. Nevertheless, his writings often show some awkward spelling and down-country way of expressing things – all of which brought him closer to the people.

His comments on and analysis of a variety of subjects in this book offer both his quick wit and his almost hayseed way of saying some things. There is no effort to clean up his way of saying things; the occasional awkward spellings are the way he said and wrote things.

It would certainly be a mistake to attempt to say something better than Will Rogers said it.

So, let's take a look at what Will might say about some things today. (All quotes with dates included are from the Telegrams, unless otherwise cited.)

--rvw

Chapter 1: Presidents

It takes more than promises. . .

"I have read all presidential speeches on both sides up to now, and the winner is the man smart enough to not make any more. There is a great chance for a 'silent' third party." (Aug. 17, 1932.)

One of Will Rogers's favorite targets was U.S. presidents. He teased the candidates when they were running for the office, and he lampooned those who succeeded in getting there.

He didn't spare the press, either, referring to an upcoming presidential talk: "I am anxious to hear the comments in the press. Even if it's good there is plenty of 'em won't like it, he can speak on the Lord's supper and get editorials against it.

"Never in our history was we as willing to blame somebody else for our troubles.

"America is just like an insane asylum. There is not a soul in it will admit they are crazy. Roosevelt being the warden at the present time, us inmates know he is the one that's cuckoo." (April 28, 1935.)

Will noticed that many so-called political experts insisted the president should guarantee the nation's prosperity. Referring to President Franklin Roosevelt, Will said:

"I can just see Mr. Roosevelt rushing in with a guarantee reading about as follows: 'Nobody guaranteed me anything when I took over this job, no man gambles more than president of the U.S., so you will pardon me if I am not able to guarantee business that it won't lose.'" (Nov. 27, 1934.)

And in his "Will Says" offerings, he has a few things to say about running for president: "There is people so excited over this election that they think the president has something to do with running the country."

"Being serious or being a good fellow has got nothing to do with running this country. If the breaks are with you, you could be a laughing hyena and still have a great administration."

"There is not a voter in America that twenty-four hours after any speech was made could remember two sentences in it."

President Barack Obama certainly had his share of critics, as he geared up in late 2011 for his re-election campaign. He was generally considered a top speaker, but often rapped for promising a lot and delivering little. (Isn't that one definition of a politician?)

"What if the president gave a major speech and no one heard it? Not a likely scenario, yet this was the question in play for several days as President Obama requested and was kinda-sorta denied an audience before a joint session of Congress. . ." – Kathleen Parker, Washington Post Writers Group, in St. Joseph News-Press, Sept. 4, 2011.

Maybe President Obama should study President Calvin Coolidge:

"As human beings gain in individual perfection so the world will gain in social perfection, and we may hope to come into an era of right thinking and right living, of good will and of peace, in accordance with the teachings of the Great Physician." (Quoted by Will Rogers in his Telegram of May 18, 1927: He added: "Gee! That sounds like one of those birthday greeting cards.")

Despite painful unemployment, bank failures and a staggering economy, President Obama continued to tell the American public how well we were doing under his leader-ship. In September 2011 he presented a new $450 billion plan designed to create new jobs and rejuvenate the economy.

"This plan is the right thing to do right now," he told Congress. "You should pass it." -- Associated Press, Sept. 11, 2011. Republicans of the opposing party cringed at the cost, when the nation was deeply in debt. The plan was still sitting there as 2011 drew to a close.

Similar words were heard by Will Rogers years earlier in a speech by President Coolidge.

"Why, say, if we are doing only just a third as well as he says we are doing, why, we wouldn't no more let him leave us, no matter what his own inclinations are. Why, I hadn't read the speech half way through till I paid a dollar down on a half dozen things I didn't need.

"We'll show the world we are prosperous if we have to go broke to do it." (Nov. 18, 1927.)

Recessions and depressions are usually blamed on the man in the White House at the time, although there are multiple factors, of course. Will thought so, too:

"Here is the best one I have seen yet. A Hollywood film extra, suing her husband for divorce, claiming it on the grounds that 'her husband accused her of being the cause of the depression.'

"That will certainly be welcome news to Mr. Hoover to know there is somebody blamed for all the world's depression besides him." (July 25, 1932.)

Sometimes Will wondered why anyone would want to be president in the first place. In a few "Will Says," he muses over this question.

"One of the evils of democracy is you have to put up with the man you elected whether you want him or not. That's why we call it democracy."

"If I was a president and wanted something I would claim I didn't want it. Congress has not given any president anything he wanted in the last 10 years. Be against anything and then he is sure to get it."

"The high office of president has been degenerated into two ordinarily fine men being goaded by political leeches into saying things that if they were in their right minds they wouldn't think of saying."

"Sometimes it makes you think we don't need a different man as much as we need different advisors for the same man."

All through recent history, it seems, the U.S. is meeting with nations somewhere to try to disarm everybody so there will be no more wars. So far it hasn't worked too well, maybe partly because all these same nations are hard at work coming up with new weapons to kill each other. Will commented on the lack of progress:

"I see by a delayed American paper that Mr. Coolidge is going to print the history of the United States on a single rock. Well, I could print the history of the present results of this disarmament conference on the head of a pin and have room enough left for the chorus of 'Yes, We Have No Bananas.'" (Feb. 4, 1930.)

Unlike some "experts," Will did not believe the way out of economic troubles was to spend more:

"If ever there was a time to save, it's now. When a dog gets a bone he don't go out and make the first payment on a larger bone with it. He buries the one he's got.

"Don't make the first payment on anything. First payments is what made us think we were prosperous, and the other nineteen is what showed us we were broke." (July 9, 1930.)

He also wondered about all these special commissions to solve our problems:

"No matter how bad the depression gets and how short we become of the necessities of life we never seem to run out of material to put on a commission. Mr. Hoover just got ahold of a book called 'Who's Who for No Reason at All' and appointed sixty men. That breaks his own record for quantity if nothing else." (Aug. 21, 1931.)

For someone who wrote a lot, including the Daily Telegrams, Will understood that too many words did not necessarily mean a good thing. He also offered some hints to any president:

"Mr. Hoover delivered his prescription to Congress yesterday on the 'condition of the country.' It was 12,000 words long. That's how bad shape we are in. And he hinted to Congress that they was the one thing that got us that way, but if they would get busy and do something at this session, he hoped to cut our 'conditions' down to maybe 6,000 by the time he enumerates our troubles again." (Dec. 4, 1929.)

Sometimes, Will noted, it's not only Congress which gives the president so much trouble:

"Poor Mr. Hoover, if things ever do turn, and start breaking right for him, he will be a good man to string with, for he ought to have a long streak of luck. Of all the things that's gone against him, the worst one happened this week. His speech run 15 minutes overtime, and he took up Amos and Andy's time on the radio.

"That was a vote loser sure enough. That did him more harm than even the Wicksersham report." (June 19, 1931.)

It's not likely that President Obama or any other president these days would agree with at least one of President Hoover's comments:

"Mr. Hoover went out to Cleveland Thursday and spoke before the bankers. I liked his speech. He didn't beat around the bush about anything. He just come out right in the opening paragraph and said he was doing pretty 'mangy.' (Of course, he might have suspected that we had already found it out.)" (Oct. 3, 1930.)

One of the big stories of the Obama administration, with more heat poured on during the jostling leading up to the 2012 presidential election, has been his troubles with Congress. Other presidents have had to struggle with – and fight – Congress during their terms, of course:

"Tomorrow is a historic day. Mr. Hoover, all during his career, has had men almost lay down their lives to aid him in carrying out some good work. That all ends tomorrow. Congress meets, and his faith in human nature will start waning before sundown." (April 14, 1929.)

President Obama seems also to have lost faith in Congress, if you can believe the news media:

"Leaving behind a year of bruising legislative battles, President Barack Obama enters his fourth year in office having calculated that he no longer needs Congress to promote his agenda and may even benefit in his re-election campaign if lawmakers accomplish little." -- Julie Pace of the Associated Press, in Kansas City Star, Jan. 1, 2012.

Will Rogers figured that presidents throughout history have had their difficulties with Congress:

"Hoover gets rid of something useless every day. Wait till he sees the Senate and Congress.

"He sunk the Mayflower without warning; he took the White House stables and made a garage for fishing poles out of it; sent six horses to the museum that had never been able to be ridden since Taft got through with them; traded the mechanical horse for a medicine ball, and makes everybody catch it before they can get any breakfast. That's to discourage Senators eating there." (March 26, 1929.)

Will Rogers also hammered at a president's need to keep prodding Congress to do something. (President Obama has learned that lesson well, but with dubious results.)

"Say, this Roosevelt is a fast worker. Even on Sunday when all a president is supposed to do is put on a silk hat and have his picture taken coming out of church, why this president closed all the banks and called Congress in extra session, and that's not all he's going to call 'em either if they don't get something done." (March 6, 1933.)

President Obama learned the lesson so well, he decided maybe the best course was to move ahead by going around Congress:

"Pushing a campaign to act without Congress, President Obama moved unilaterally Friday to boost private business. . . Obama ordered direct government agencies to shorten the time it takes for federal research to turn into commercial products in the marketplace. . ." --Associated Press in St. Joseph News-Press, Oct. 11, 2011.

Will also suggested that a president would understand the problems of the common man better if he would just try their situations himself. Referring to President Coolidge, he said:

"Put him on a farm with the understanding he has to make his own living of it, and I bet he will give the farmers relief next year. I offer mine for the experiment, and if he makes a go of it he is not a president, he is a magician." (March 9, 1927.)

Will could not resist using an otherwise damaging event to point out how well commissions work:

"The White House fire burned quite awhile due to the following: When Mr. Hoover discovered that 'some kind of condition existed' he sent out letters inviting all the Fire Departments in Washington, and when they arrived appointed them on a commission 'to investigate, and recommend remedies.'

They did investigate, and on account of there being no prominent businessmen on the commission, they turned in their report fairly quick. 'We find a fire does exist, and in keeping with the spirit of every amendment, recommend nothing but water to extinguish it.'

"Of course, by this time the house had burned down, but it was nevertheless gratifying to Mr. Hoover, for it was the first commission that he had ever appointed in his life that had really ever turned in a report. So he figures the loss of the building well worth it. It will renew his faith in commissions." (Dec. 26, 1929.)

As a newspaper columnist, Will Rogers was always looking for a way to beat other newsmen to a story. He used just such an opportunity to give an insight into President Coolidge, famous for using few words:

"Mr. Coolidge, what is your impression of the general condition of our country?"

"Mr. Coolidge – Yes."

"How long do you think the disarmament conference will last?"

"No."

"Is this tinkering with the tariff good for the country as a whole?"

"Meby."

"What do you think of the way the Senate has formed this obstructive coalition?"

"Uh."

"What's the president going to do about this prohibition amendment?"

"Huh."

"Who is the logical candidate in case Mr. Hoover don't care for another term?"

"Uh huh."

"Will you have another biscuit, Mr. Coolidge?"

"Probably."

(Feb. 20, 1930.

Various experts among the news media love to jump on different politicians about all sorts of things. Sometimes they are even right, at least in part. President Obama turned out to be a popular target.

The Obama administration had announced a new "strategy" of urging citizens to go on-line with their issues so the government could solve their problems. They promised significant results.

"Doesn't it drive you crazy when elected officials say they're going to do something and then don't? Worse is when they kinda-sorta do something to pretend they've made an impact, as if no one's going to notice that they really haven't." -- Esther J. Cepeda, Washington Post Writers Group, in St. Joseph News-Press Nov. 4, 2011.

Will Rogers liked to point out that different presidents came up with various plans like Obama's:

"Mr. Hoover wants to put in the 'stagger system.' That don't sound like a dry.

"He says we can save eighty million a year by 'staggering.' We have always thought 'staggering' was a shame, but now it's a blessing.

"But what he means by the 'stagger' is you 'stagger' to work today, then 'stagger' home and lay off tomorrow, and I 'stagger' over and work in your place that day, then you 'stagger' back the next day.

"The man who is employing you don't know just who is going to 'stagger' in to work for him on any given day, but it gives more people days to work and more people days to 'stagger,' so the plan is well worth 'staggering' into." (April 17, 1932.)

Sometimes Will found a president's words fascinating:

"My advice to Mr. Coolidge on preparedness is slowly bearing fruit. Here are his exact words in a speech Saturday: 'What we need and all that we do need for national protection is adequate protection.'

"Couldn't ask for a clearer statement that that. What a hungry man needs and all that he needs for personal sustenance is adequate food and shelter. All even a Democrat needs for self-presentation is adequate votes." (Jan. 30, 1927.)

Sometimes, though, he felt a little sympathy for a president:

"See where some society visiting President Hoover said for humane reasons they didn't have him shake hands with them. Well, that was fine. Now, why didn't they go further with their good idea and not visit him and take up his time? Then they would have been 100 per cent correct." (April 25, 1929.)

Will could even find some historical precedent:

"President Hoover made a mighty fine and very sincere speech Saturday at Valley Forge. He found somebody that was worse off than we are, but he had to go back 150 years in history to do it.

"He claims that George Washington was in just about as bad shape with his Army then as Mellon is with his deficit now.

"But George only had to worry about getting through the winter. We got to worry about getting through the Summer, then the Winter, then another Summer before the Democrats can possibly do anything for us." (May 31, 1931.)

In Will's day, just as now, the U.S. government was concerned about debt (well, it would be nice if Congress would be concerned about it). Will had a solution:

"Mr. Hoover is stealing my act. He wants to postpone international debts for a year. Two weeks ago I had the same scheme, only I took more territory, I wanted to cancel everbody's, and every nation's debt, and the only person that fell for my plan was two guys that owed me. They immediately agreed and canceled." (June 21, 1931.)

Will Rogers seemed to sit back and wait to see what happened during presidential election campaigns. He did have comments from time to time about candidates, though:

"Been reading Sunday's casualty lists from automobiles. It looks like everybody gets run over but presidential candidates. Is there no justice in the world?" ("Will Says.")

President Obama revved up the campaign furor and lighted another fire under critics when he blocked a proposed pipeline which would provide oil from Canada to the U.S.

"The Obama administration on Wednesday rejected, for now, the controversial Keystone XL pipeline, igniting a gusher of outrage from those championing the $7 billion project as a jobs creator and a means to lessen U.S. reliance on foreign oil." (Donald Bradley in the Kansas City Star, Jan. 19, 2012.)

This sort of action by a U.S. president prompted Will Rogers to address actions of a president during a campaign.

"Don't you all kinder wish that the president of our country wouldn't have to run around all over the land getting upon a soap box to shout his merits like a backwoods Congressman running for re-election?

"That's why a president's term should be six years; no re-election, and be retired for life on half salary. Then he serves with dignity right up to the finish. And don't have to take part in this mess of promises, accusations and ballyhoo.

"We thought when the radio was perfected and everybody could hear a speech, that it wouldn't be necessary to drag a president around over the country like a circus. But, no, the state leaders must satisfy their vanity by having him appear 'in person' in their state.

"But, after all, there is very little dignity, very little sportsmanship, or very little anything in politics, only 'get the job and hold it.'" (Nov. 2, 1932.)

Now if there were ever a statement as true today as it was in 1932, that's it right there.

Political campaigns, especially those involving presidential hopefuls, seem to open the spigots of nasty accusations, dirty laundry and other unpleasant things.

In 2012 the campaigning sometimes became really nasty, as candidates insulted each other. And that was just on the Republican side – the main race between the two parties hadn't even started yet. Even the candidates themselves sometimes stopped and took at hard look at what was going on:

"This race has degenerated into an onslaught of negative and personal attacks not worthy of the American people and not worthy of this critical time in our nation's history." (Republican candidate Jon Huntsman, quoted in Time magazine, Jan. 30, 2012.)

It wasn't always like that, according to Will:

"George Washington was a politician and a gentleman. That's a rare combination." ("Will Says.")

In recent years presidents and their families have made many trips at home and overseas, and often they take an astonishing number of staff people with them. (We, the taxpayers, pay for this, don't we?) But this, too, is not something new. Will Rogers commented on something like this many years ago:

"Our president left for a quiet vacation with twelve carloads of cameramen, reporters, cooks, valets, maids, butlers, doctors, military and naval attaches. I saw King George when he left Buckingham Palace in London last Summer for his vacation, and you could have put all he and Mary both had in a Ford truck.

"We ain't got exactly what you would call a corner on democracy." (June 15, 1927.)

Much of 2012 (and too much of 2011) in the U.S. was occupied with candidates jostling for nomination to the presidency. Obama, of course, has no problem getting the Democratic nomination for reelection. But the Republicans have been fighting bitterly over their choice. Will took a slightly different angle on this situation:

"I liked Senator Curtis's announcement in the papers this morning better than any presidential ones we have had.

"He said he would accept it if he was elected, but that he wouldn't accept the nomination unless he was elected. I think that's a most straightforward and clear-sighted decision. If more men wouldn't run for offices unless they can get 'em we would have fewer races and politics would improve a thousand per cent." (Oct. 27, 1927.)

Even Will Rogers himself got into the presidential act (some presidential hopefuls might take note):

"There was a piece in the paper this morning where somebody back home was seriously proposing me for president. Now when that was done as a joke it was all right, but when it's done seriously it's just pathetic. We are used to having everything named as presidential candidates, but the country hasn't quite got to the professional comedian stage." (Feb. 2, 1928.)

He even lamented the fact that needling presidents and Congress had limits:

"Since the whole country is all agreed that we are headed toward the feed trough, and since the members of Congress have been so fine and decent and the Senators have taken out United States citizenship papers and swore allegiance to our land, and since the bankers have finally seen the errors of their ways and started banking instead of gambling, there just ain't much left for a poor writer to pick on." (April 16, 1933.)

As the campaigns heated up for the 2012 presidential election, President Obama as the incumbent had the Democratic nomination wrapped up. He must have enjoyed watching the Republican candidates rip each other to shreds in bitter state primaries. Several candidates dropped out after early primaries, and in later January it really became nasty.

"The race for the Republican presidential nomination took a turn toward the South Carolina surreal Thursday as Rick Perry dropped out, Newt Gingrich faced stunning allegations from an ex-wife and Mitt Romney struggled to maintain a shaky front-runner's standing." (David Espo of the Associated Press in St. Joseph News-Press, Jan. 20, 2012.)

Chapter 2: America and Americans

Who are we?

"A big step forward in modern civilization was made last night here in Los Angeles (the last place you would expect civilization to advance). It was a dinner given at $100 a plate, with the distinct understanding there would be no speeches. The place was sold out and everybody tickled to death. The funds from the dinner were divided among those who wanted to make speeches but were not allowed. Everyone in the hall received $100." (May 16, 1928.)

Even though Will Rogers liked to portray himself as just an old country boy or cowboy, he couldn't resist sampling philosophy from time to time. It's truly remarkable how some things he said years ago apply right now:

"Actual knowledge of the future was never lower, but hope was never higher.

"Confidence will beat predictions any time." ("Will Says.")

He could get right to the point without the need for a lot of long-winded babble:

"Everybody is ignorant. Only on different subjects."

One of the things that made Will Rogers so popular was his insistence on being one of the common people, despite his fame and worldwide following:

"Nothing makes people more alike than putting a dress suit on 'em."

"Half our life is spent trying to find something to do with the time we have rushed through life trying to save."

Back in the early 1930s, the United States was going through some really tough economic times, just as we are in 2012. And just as now, a lot of the blame was placed on Congress and the bankers.

Will often looked at Americans with an amusing tolerance:

"The American people are a very generous people and will forgive almost any weakness, with the possible exception of stupidity."

He also thought that maybe Americans are a little too gullible sometimes:

"You can take a sob story and a stick of candy and lead America right off into the Dead Sea."

For the umpteenth time, Congress again has been arguing (without getting anywhere – also for the umpteenth time) over immigration and how to solve that problem. Some in Congress, of course, did not see any problem. Will Rogers had a solution for at least part of the immigration problem:

"Papers say 60,000 Filipinos want to go home. Well, you can't blame a person for being homesick, and fare is cheaper than relief.

"Why wouldn't that be a good move for the government to make, send anybody home that wants to go, or any American citizen that craves a change. (They say citizenship here now is not so hot.)

"So while everybody is introducing a bill, or a plan, the Rogers plan read as follows:

"'Party of the first part (the U.S.A.) will ship anybody, anywhere, if they won't come back.'" (Feb. 25, 1935.)

People today are always in a hurry. Well, they were in a hurry in Will's day, too:

"There never was such a demand for speed, for less reason.

There is not a one of us that couldn't walk where we are going and then get there earlier than we have any business."

Sometimes Will even strayed from his cowboy philosophy and became downright serious:

"You can't legislate any common sense into people. You can't broaden a man's vision if he wasn't born with one."

Along with his unending looks into what makes things tick, Will was the eternal optimist. He sort of liked to let everyone know that things would get better, no matter how bad it looked at the moment.

"All we hear is 'What's the matter with the world?' There ain't but one thing wrong with every one of us in the world, and that's selfishness."

And he could steer you away from really serious stuff, to something maybe serious to some but still enough to give you a laugh.

"Somebody is always quoting figures to prove that the country is prosperous, and it takes a lot of quoting; but the only real bona fide indication of it was in the paper today: 'Divorces in Reno have increased over 105 per cent in the last year.'

"Now, that's prosperity, for you can't be broke and get a divorce. That's why the poor have to live with each other. There is nothing that denotes prosperity quicker than to hear that 'so and so and his wife ain't getting along.'

"I maintain that it should cost as much to get married as it does to get divorced. Make it look like marriage is worth as much as a divorce, even if it ain't. That would also make the preachers financially independent like it has the lawyers." (May 15, 1928.)

But even with his focus on everyday life, Will liked to tinker with genuine philosophy sometimes:

Robert V. Waldrop

"Humanity is not yet ready for either real truth or real harmony."

And he could deal with the personal side, too:

"A fanatic is always the fellow that is on the opposite side."

"A man can fool you with his mind, and his Soul and his Heart, but if you follow his feet you will pretty near find out where he is going."

Comments like these put Will in the same class with more famous philosophers, who also would tell us what the universe is about and how you define truth and important stuff like that.

But Will liked to narrow down this serious philosophy stuff to the guy next door, or maybe the pompous clunk in the news who you somehow just could not like.

"The minute a fellow gets into the Chamber of Commerce, he quits mowing his own lawn."

"Nothing will spoil a big man's life like too much truth."

"I can remember when a man could be considered respectable without belonging to a golf club."

But Will never forgot his country roots:

"A man in the country does his own thinking. Get him into town and he will be thinking second-hand."

"The world is full of men who do big things, but when you meet 'em they are not outstanding personalities. Pretty near everybody is almost alike."

"You can look at half the guy's stomachs in the world, and you can see they don't know how to order for themselves."

Time and time again Will took the optimistic view toward life:

"There is nothing as easy as denouncing. It don't take much to see that something is wrong but it does take some eyesight to see what will put it right again."

18

But even Will Rogers couldn't help but admit that some things, and some people, don't seem to belong in the same barnyard with the other animals:

"Nobody wants his cause near as bad as he wants to talk about his cause."

"The thing of being a hero, about the main thing to do is to know when to die. Prolonged life has ruined more men that it ever made."

"Modern history has proven that there has never been a will left that was carried out exactly as the maker of the money intended."

And he didn't leave himself out of thoughts like that:

"I certainly know that a comedian can only last till he either takes himself serious or his audience takes him serious, and I don't want either one of those to happen to me till I am dead (if then)."

"Nothing makes a man broad-minded like adversity."

When you get right down to it, it's the man himself that really matters, Will insisted.

"It's not what you pay a man but what he costs you that counts."

"Nothing as stupid as an educated man if you get him off the thing he was educated on."

"The fellow sitting off looking at you can tell better how you are doing and what your prospects are than you can yourself."

America's role in world affairs continues to be a popular topic among the "experts." Some say we should play a stronger role in world affairs, others say we should mind our own business. Nobody knows the right answer.

Froma Harrop, a columnist for Creators Syndicate, wrote in the Nov. 11, 2011, St. Joseph News-Press:

"A perceived decline in 'national greatness' haunts Americans of all political persuasions. Many equate it with the drop in our superpower status. But others ask, 'Are the costs of perpetually commanding the high ground worth it?'. . ."

She is probably right. But maybe Will Rogers said it just as well, and a lot quicker:

"This would be a great time in the world for some man to come along that knew something."

He had a few other things to say about civilization and getting along with others:

"We will never have true civilization until we have learned to recognize the rights of others."

"What all of us know put together don't mean anything. Nothing don't mean anything. We are here for a spell and pass on. Anyone who thinks that civilization has advanced is an egotist."

And Will would not back away from offering a few good-living tips:

"If you live right, death is a joke to you as far as fear is concerned."

"The Lord split knowledge up among his subjects about equal. The so-called ignorant is happy. You think he is happy because he don't know any better. Maybe he is happy because he knows enough to be happy. The smart one knows a lot. That makes him unhappy because he can't impart it to his friends. Discontent comes in proportion to knowledge."

"Education never helped morals. The most savage people are the most moral. The smarter the guy the bigger the rascal."

Prohibition was a big issue in Will's day, and his native state of Oklahoma teetered (he would have said staggered) on the question. From time to time he brought up the question of legal drinking (illegal drinking was never a problem in Oklahoma):

"Well, here we are, flying out of Tulsa, the first town in America to become a city. This is one of the best and busiest airports in our country. Oklahoma wants to vote on the beer thing, but they have no money to pay for the election, so Missouri offers to pay for Oklahoma's election provided Oklahoma will guarantee to vote dry and let them have the sales privilege as they do now." (May 12, 1933.)

Years earlier, he reported on the situation in Oklahoma:

"Leaving the glorious State of Oklahoma tonight by popular demand.

"The South is dry and will vote dry. That is, everybody that is sober enough to stagger to the polls will." (Oct. 28, 1926.)

Sometimes Will tried to explain to the rest of the world what the status of prohibition really was:

"Prohibition is never an issue in the South, their habits and their votes have nothing in common. They feel they are the originators of the still, and any legislation to permit large breweries would be unfair competition and would perhaps destroy the entire revenue of hundreds of thousands of small still owners, who have no other visible means of support. Corn likker is their product, and I can't blame them for voting to protect its life.

"You see, you must not condemn a people until you have been among them and can see and know their angle. I don't blame them for not wanting big corporation breweries to be allowed by law to try and change their tastes. We would be a fine liberty-loving country if we allowed a few Yankees to dictate to us what we could make and what we could drink.

"Prohibition isn't an issue down here; it's a privilege." (Oct. 16, 1926.)

This question of prohibition wasn't limited, in Will's view, to just his home state, of course:

"Oklahoma, Al Smith is coming down there tomorrow, and I want the old home to treat him right. He has been good to lots of us back here [Will was in New York at the time]. Don't pull off any snipe shooting or badger fights, don't even break his derby. Show him the State produces something besides outlaws, bo-weevil and comedians.

"Tell him what a great territory we had before we struck oil and Republicans, followed by mortgages, foreclosures and impeachments." (Sept. 18, 1928.)

Even the president at the time got into the act:

"Hoover appoints ten lawyers and one woman to see if anybody is drinking and why.

"If President Hoover thinks there is ten men drinking to every woman, then we will appoint a commission to look into his case. Well, it's up to the lone woman to do something. I can think of nothing that the people would have less confidence in than ten lawyers put together.

"It does look like he could have appointed one fellow with just horse sense." (May 21, 1929.)

Will even brought modern science into the discussion:

"Say, these scientists and chemists are getting smart. They got some kind of a concoction called the 'black light.' The prohibition authorities have already bought the exclusive right. If you have been drinking, they can give you a swig of their dope on top of yours and immediately your innards loom up like a bulletin board. It registers the brand of stuff you have been drinking, the city it comes from, the color of the bootlegger's hair and the price you paid. If it's in Oklahoma City, the Jamaica ginger will loom up like you was going to bake a cake. So if you see a dry officer coming, don't only hide the bottle, but conceal your stomach." (March 11, 1930.)

Once he even brought a famous sports figure, heavyweight boxer Gene Tunney, into the discussion:

"Did you see this morning's paper where Gene Tunney was drinking beer in Paris and said he didn't drink beer at home because our home brew was terrible?

"Now listen, Gene, you can criticize our boxing skill, you can make light of our intellect, you can denounce us as morons, but don't make light of our home brew. You are condemning the very spirit of our American homes. It's made by hand, not by factory. We have had nine years' practice and we don't want to be told we can't learn anything in that time.

"So stick to your books. You may know Shakespeare, but you don't know our beer." (Sept. 10, 1928.)

One year Will came up with a unique way to express Christmas wishes. People and companies today would do well to consider his idea:

"There must be an awful lot of factories and firms and individuals that have always been shown some kind of appreciation to their folks on Xmas who perhaps this year, on account of conditions, are not able to do all they would like to and are at a loss just what to do.

"Wouldn't this be more welcome than a gift? Send each one a note and tell 'em they are not going to be fired, that their position is secure.

"I believe that will be a mighty acceptable Xmas present to everybody that is on salary. It will beat any present you can send, relieve their anxiety and let them go out and do some shopping on their own, and thereby help everybody.

"We are bad off, but the world ain't coming to an end yet." (Dec. 16, 1930.)

If those comments sound like Will cared about his fellow humans, well, he did.

In an earlier Christmas message, he had a different but thoughtful look at Christmas, after it was over:

"Well, the Xmas spirit is over now. Everybody can get back to their natural dispositions. If there had been as many good wishes in the heart as there was on paper the devil would have to dig up some new clients.

"Christmas will never be a real charity event till we learn to eat those Xmas cards. If we spent as much with the Salvation Army as we do with the telegraph companies every Xmas, why the poor would be fat all Winter.

"But we can all go back to work with a clear conscience. We fed 'em Xmas and New Year's; now all the poor have to do is just fill in the few meals till next Xmas." (Dec. 25, 1928.)

Will often traveled about the nation, and he also made trips abroad. But he was always glad to get back home. When he returned after one such trip to Europe, he wrote:

"Oh, boy, I was glad to set my old big feet on American soil, even if it has got a second mortgage on it.

"Had the greatest trip I ever had in my life and I believe if everybody made it they might come back poorer but better off in the feeling toward our country.

"I know business is off, they say 60 per cent. Well, that still leaves us 30 per cent ahead of anywhere I have seen.

"If we can just let other people alone and let them do their own fighting. When you get into trouble 5,000 miles away from home, you've got to have been looking for it." (Feb. 9, 1932.)

He also had another memory from his trip:

"A bunch of American tourists were hissed and stoned yesterday in France but not until they had finished buying."

"No nation ever had two better friends than we have. You know who they are? The Atlantic and Pacific oceans."

In a philosophical vein again:

"You can't have a picnic unless the party carrying the basket comes."

"Popularity is the easiest thing in the world to gain and it is the hardest thing to hold."

"I think the same fellow who started that self-made man gag started that other asinine expression, '100 per cent American.' Every human from the time he is weaned is self-made. And how do you know when a man is made anyhow? He may be only partly finished when a lot of guys call him made."

After California endured one of its many earthquakes, Will had to tell his readers about it:

"Bless Arthur Brisbane's loyal heart, he tried to say it wasn't an earthquake. He said the buildings were non-union construction and the people were killed through a sudden stroke of old age.

"But he didn't know that our California papers had turned frank and just said:

"'We had an earthquake. It was no fire, no tidal wave, no act of Democratic party, it was just an old fashioned earthquake.

"You see the Lord in his justice works everything on a handicap basis. California having the best of everything else must take a slice of the calamities. Even my native Oklahoma (the Garden of Eden of the West) has a cyclone. Kansas, while blessed with its grasshoppers, must endure its politicians. New York with its splendor has its Wall Street, and Washington, the world's most beautiful city, has a lobbyist crawling out to attack you from every manhole."

Writing from a visit to a ranch near Ponca City, Okla., Will mentioned some queen was about to visit:

"Am at Miller Brothers' 101 Ranch just ahead of the Queen's visit here. She will love it. It's just the size of Rumania, only more conveniences. There is a bathroom here to every revolution there. Cowboys sleep in silk pajamas, round-up in Rolls-Royces and dress for dinner. If I were the King I wouldn't trust her with this outfit."

A few more philosophical tidbits:

"A man only learns by two things, one is reading, and the other is association with smarter people."

"Call me a 'rube' and a 'hick,' but I'd lot rather be the man who bought the Brooklyn Bridge than the man who sold it."

"The more you know the more you think somebody owes you a living."

"Just signed up for the coming sorority hop is those ex-White House coeds, Mrs. Benjamin Harrison, Mrs. Theodore Roosevelt, Mrs. William Howard Taft, Mrs. Calvin Coolidge and Mrs. Herbert Hoover. And nothing is any more gratifying to America than to welcome back into the fold all those gracious and sturdy American women.

"Funny thing about that White House. It wears down the most hardy of our men folks, but the women seem to thrive on it." (Oct. 11, 1934.)

Chapter 3: Congress

These people influence our lives. . .

"Every year it gets harder and harder to tell the difference between a Republican and a Democrat. (Course outside of the looks.)

"Their platforms and policies become more and more alike. But I believe I have found out the sure way to tell one from another this year. It's just the way they talk. The Republican says, 'Well, things could have been worse,' and the Democrat says, 'How?'" (Aug. 5, 1932.)

As the year 2012 gained steam, many experts once again proclaimed the year to be a historical turning point for our nation. It's happened before, of course. The main contest was for president, but members of Congress were under intensive fire for failure to solve the nation's problems. It was a "lame duck" Congress, meaning an unknown number of members would serve for a few months after they were ousted in the November election.

"An awful lot of people are confused as to just what is meant by a 'lame duck Congress.'

"It's like when some fellows worked for you and their work wasn't satisfactory and you let 'em out, you let 'em stay long enough so they could burn your house down.

"You know Ruth Bryan Owen, the Congresswoman who had always been a prohibitionist and was defeated in the primary on it. You got to give her credit. When she saw that the vote was against it, why she held no revenge, but voted with the repealists.

"So, there you have a woman with more nerve than a lot of men." (Dec. 8. 1932.)

But one never knows how a Congressman will vote, does one?

"Everybody is knocking this lame-duck Congress, but do you know those fellows have a chance to make a real name for themselves and make us ashamed that we fired 'em.

"They know exactly how the people voted on every question that they will be asked to decide on. They know the majority didn't want prohibition. They know the majority don't want the debt canceled. They know everybody wants government expense cut in half.

"So when any questions comes all they have to do is read the election returns. Course, if they still want to be on the minority side of all these things we will know exactly why they was defeated." (Dec. 4, 1932.)

And then, the game began, just as it will again in 2012. Once again the voters will find out which Congressmen vote the way the voters want them to vote.

"Congress opened today. It's called the lame duck session. A lame duck is a politician who is still alive, but the government paymaster has been notified that he will become totally disabled on March 4.

"Today's session was very congenial. They met, prayed, and adjourned. But wait till the Boulder Dam bill comes up. Then the City of Washington will get a shock to its national pride. They will find that the power lobby didn't just settle there on account of the beauty of the charming city. We shall soon discover the susceptible." (Dec. 3, 1928.)

One of Will Rogers's observations which was right on target, at least according to many financial experts, was the one about having money to pay for things. He could have been addressing the Congress of 2012:

"The worst thing that has happened to us in a long time is that this is an election year. Every statesman wants to vote appropriations, but is afraid to vote taxes. The oratory of Washington is on 'reconstruction,' but the heart of Washington is on November 4, 1932.

"We never will get anywhere with our finances till we pass a law saying that every time we appropriate something we got to pass another bill along with it stating where the money is coming from." (Feb. 12, 1932.)

Maybe the Congress of 2012 faces even bigger obstacles. According to some news sources, there is not much respect in the nation for the Congress of 2011-2012:

"Consider this: An Associated Press-GfK poll released nine days ago indicated that only 12 percent of Americans think positively about Congress." (Ken Newton in the St. Joseph News-Press, Sept. 11, 2011.)

A month earlier Laurie Kellman and Jennifer Agiesta in an Associated Press story voiced similar thoughts:

"To be sure, there is plenty of discontent to go around. The poll finds more people are down on their own member of Congress, not just the institution, an unusual finding in surveys and one bound to make incumbents particularly nervous." (AP, Aug. 11, 2011.)

Will Rogers would not argue:

"Congressmen are coming dragging in from Washington. Some of 'em look like they had hitchhiked.

"Now their real work starts. That is trying to get elected this fall. I tell you it's no easy life when you consider that battle to get back there.

"I just don't know what they are going to promise the voters this fall. This is a tough time to think up something new. About a man's only chance is to just say, 'Well, boys, I don't know what I will do. I will just have to wait till I get there and see what Mr. Roosevelt wants. He knows more about it than me." (June 26, 1934.)

There wasn't too much hope once they got back there:

"The regular session of Congress opened today to investigate what was done at the last session.

"This session is also to relieve the farmer again – to relieve him of any encouragement that he might have received during the last one.

"One thing – Mr. Hoover is not responsible for the holding of this session. Got to blame the founders of the Constitution for it. Can't lay this one on him. That last one cured him." (Dec. 2, 1929.)

It's a funny thing – no, maybe "sad" is a better word – how some problems don't ever seem to change:

"Congress is human for the first time in years. They are broke, just like everybody else, and are running around in a circle trying to pay what they owe.

"They got an 18-billion-dollar first plaster on the country, and now they are popeyed trying to get a second mortgage. They will eventually find out they are just like other folks; they will have to cut down." (May 20, 1932.)

This recurring trend is not limited to national finances. In 2011 the nation suffered devastating floods, and Will Rogers commented on how Congress coped with flood relief decades earlier:

"Just passed through the lower Mississippi flood district again, first time since last May. Congress has taken up the tariff, farm relief, big navy, Al Smith, Ku Klux, Nicaragua, Cuban independence, Mexico oil, Boulder Dam and Tom Heflin, but nothing has been said about building the dikes higher. They will wait till the night they adjourn and then pass a resolution against another flood." (Jan. 23, 1928.)

Sometimes Will thought Congress represented a challenge – to him:

"I been working day and night since almost yesterday with this fellow Johnson on a code for comedians. He claims that Senators and Congressmen come under our code. I claim theirs is a separate union, that they are professionals and in a class by themselves and that us amateur comedians should not be classed with 'em.

"I hate to defy this NRA, but I am going to carry my fight to the country, because, according to his code, it would give more work to Senators and Congressmen, and I claim that's the only thing we don't want any more of." (Aug. 18, 1933.)

Maya MacGuineas, president of the nonpartisan Committee for a Responsible Federal Budget, was quoted in the Dec. 5, 2011, issue of Time magazine:

"Never underestimate the willingness of politicians to try to avoid making some of the hard choices."

Meanwhile, Will Rogers kept his eye on Congress:

"Went up to the 'opera comique' and heard the cast argue in both houses. Senator Thomas, from our great old State of Oklahoma, was trying to get a little appropriation for the Indians. Vice President Curtis and I were the only two that applauded. It's tough to get help for even the little white brothers, much less us Injuns." (Jan. 21, 1931.)

Money matters seem to pose a problem for every Congress, and they come up with some strange solutions:

"Congress knocked the rich in the creek with a 72 per cent income tax, and then somebody must have told 'em, 'Yes, Congress you got 'em when they are living. But what if they die on you to keep from paying it?'

"Congress says, 'Well, never thought of that, so we will frame one that will get 'em, alive or living, dead or deceased.'

"Now they got such a high inheritance tax on 'em that you won't catch these old rich boys dying promiscuously like they did.

"This bill makes patriots out of everybody. You sure do die for your country if you die from now on." (March 23, 1932.)

Well, what about the income tax? Doesn't Congress always show restraint and good sense when dealing with taxes on the common people?

"Secretary Mellon has asked Congress to please wait till after March 15, when the new income taxes come in, before passing any legislation, as he don't know how much there will be, if any.

"But Congress says, 'No, we are going to divide it up now, whether there is any to divide or not. What do you suppose we are in Congress for, it if ain't to split up the swag? Please pass the gravy." (Jan. 1, 1928.)

Speaking of our hard-working Congress, Will addressed Congress and their hard work, or labor:

"Tomorrow is Labor Day (I suppose set by an act of Congress). Everything we do nowadays is either by or against act of Congress.

"How Congress knew anything about labor is beyond us, but anyhow tomorrow is Labor Day. It's a day in the big cities where men march all day and work harder than they have in any other of the 365. Even the ones that ain't working labor on Labor Day.

"There is two things that tickle the fancy of our citizens, one is let him act on a committee, and the other is promise him to let him walk in a parade.

"What America needs is to get more mileage out of our parades." (Sept. 1, 1929.)

There probably was never anyone who needled our nation's politicians more than Will Rogers. Despite this, he seemed to get along with most of them, and many even said they enjoyed his comments.

"Say, you all got to quit knocking Congress. Didn't you see what they did yesterday? Passed a bill to cut their own salaries. Come on, let's give the boys a great hand. That was mighty good of 'em at that.

"Well, how did your taxes work today? This was the first day of the new taxes. Everybody is wondering how they come to tax the articles that they did. Well, I found out how it was done. They give each member permission to bring in the name of some article that he particularly didn't like personally, and they put a tax on for him." (June 21, 1932.)

Don't hold your breath in 2012 (or any other year), waiting for Congress to cut their own salaries. But they do look at taxes:

"Congress ought to really get into main show next week. This past week was just the overture. They will get settled down this coming week to 'steady taxing.'

"All the 'lobbies' are gathered in there to see that the tax is put on somebody else's business, but not on theirs.

"Congress got all their committees made up last week and they are composed of two Democrats to each one Republican, so what a pleasant year that poor fellow will be in for.

"Course, there is an awful lot of different breeds of Democrats. I bet you before the session is over President Roosevelt will trade you two or three Democrats for one Republican." (Jan. 13, 1935.)

"You wire the state or the federal government that your cow

or dog is sick and they will send out experts from Washington and appropriate money to eradicate the cause. You wire them that your baby has the diphtheria or scarlet fever and see what they do. . . why can't we get a government to at least do for a child's protection, what they do for a cow or a dog?" ("Will Says.")

The same problems come up all the time. Today we face terrible unemployment; too many families are struggling, and the government doesn't seem to have any answers. It's not something new:

"What's all the scandal today? Good deal of talk of Congress meeting early on account of the unemployed. Well, I believe if I was unemployed and hungry I would want a little more substantial help than just the thought of 'our boys' being gathered in Washington. In fact, I believe a man can get just as hungry with them there as he can if they are investigating the Philippines or France or somewhere else, and I am sure Mr. Hoover ain't bringing the lads in just because he has missed 'em so. But Congress might do something. They are about due." (Aug. 18, 1931.)

You've got to give them credit, though; no problem escapes close scrutiny by our Congressmen:

"A bipartisan collection of lawmakers in both houses of Congress wants legislation passed that prevents the Environmental Protection Agency from regulating dust stirred in farm fields and along rural roads." (Ken Newton in the St. Joseph News-Press, Oct. 11, 2011.)

Will Rogers noticed this attention to duty by Congress also:

"Tax relief, farm relief, flood relief, dam relief – none of these have been settled, but they are getting them in shape for consideration at the next session of Congress with the hope that those needing relief will perhaps have conveniently died in the meantime." ("Will Says.")

"Congress meets tomorrow morning. Let us all pray, Oh, Lord, give us strength to bear that which is about to be inflicted upon us. Be merciful with them, Oh Lord, for they know not what they are doing. Amen." (Dec. 5, 1926.)

But at least Will paid credit where it was due:

"Most people and actors appearing on the stage have some writer to write their material. Congress is good enough for me. They have been writing my material for years."

Members of Congress do stay busy. Most of the time nobody is sure what they are doing, or why, but they do seem to stay busy.

"In an effort many 9-year-olds will cheer, Congress wants pizza and French fries to stay on school lunch lines and is fighting the Obama administration's efforts to take unhealthy foods out of schools." (Mary Clare Jalonick of the Associated Press, in St. Joseph News-Press, Nov. 16, 2011.)

On the other hand, there are those who would insist that Congress does not accomplish too much, at least not much that the public needs or wants:

"I am here for relief. You got to come and get it personally. You can't do it through your Senator or Congressman. They are worse off than we are. Times are so hard, they are allowing constituents in their private lunch rooms to buy their Representatives meals.

"Congress hasn't done anything in so long that even the lobbyists that work on commissions are starving and hollering for personal aid. Congress yesterday turned down the 15 million food bill, and passed 15 million 'to improve entrances to national parks.' You can get a road anywhere you want to our of the government, but you can't get a sandwich.

"Well, in two years there won't be a poor farm that won't have a concrete road leading up to it." (Jan. 15, 1931.)

"Remember, write to your Congressman. Even if he can't read, write to him."

"If we could just send the same bunch of men to Washington for the good of the nation and not for political reasons, we could have the most perfect government in the world."

With so much criticism about the lack of any sensible action out of Congress, a fair question might be: Just what does Congress do, anyhow?

"Statistics have proven that the surest way to get anything out of the public mind and never hear of it again is to have a Senate Committee appointed to look into it."

"Outside of traffic, there is nothing that has held this country back as much as committees."

"Why sleep at home when you can sleep in Congress?"

Okay, maybe that's not fair. They do vote on something from time to time.

"You know how Congress is. They'll vote for anything if the thing they vote for will turn around and vote for them."

Sometimes they reach a stalemate.

"Papers say: 'Congress is deadlocked and can't act.' I think that is the greatest blessing that could befall this country."

"Didn't you see a headline in this morning's papers saying that 'Russia is going to extract the snow from the clouds before the clouds reach Moscow, thereby relieving the city of having snow'?

"Now that sounds silly, don't it? We all say, 'Those darn Russians, they always got some crazy ideas.'

"Then, in the next column it says 'Hoover and a congressional committee propose to take two hundred million dollars from government expenditure.'

"Well, I'll bet you the Russians get the snow out of the clouds before Hoover and Congress gets any government employees out of their swivel chairs." (April 10, 1932.)

All sorts of important and downright silly things are put in the Congressional Record. It's the official record of what goes on in Congress every day. One time a Congressman even mentioned Will Rogers:

"A gentleman quoted me on the floor the other day. Another member took exception and said he objected to the remarks of Professional Joke Maker going into the Congressional Record. They are the Professional Joke Makers. Read some of bills that they have passed. If you don't think they ain't Joke Makers. I could study all my life and not think up half the amount of funny things they can think of in one Session of Congress."

But Will wasn't really unhappy that he was mentioned.

"The biggest praise that a humorist can have is to get your stuff in The Congressional Record. Just think, my name will be right alongside all those other big humorists."

Sometimes it seems as if Congress just wanders around doing nothing, or nothing important.

"Well, Congress thought they knew more about how to run the country that the president so the president decided to go fishing. The trouble is the wrong one went fishing.

"So, if they bring each one of the brain trusters up to ask 'em questions, and them being all college men, those Congressmen that ask 'em the questions will have to do it through an interpreter." (March 28, 1933.)

"Just raid the national treasury enough and you will soon be referred to as a 'statesman.'"

But sooner or later, Congress will call a recess and go home or take some long "official" trip at taxpayers' expense. This is always true as the time gets closer for one of those nominating conventions.

"Congress and the Senate are wondering if they will be through in time for their various conventions.

"Now the question arises in our time, the same as in Shakespeare's (or some other old timer), 'to be in session or not to be in session, that is the question; whether it is better to suffer with or without Congress and the Senate.'

"Most folks say, 'Let them suffer like they made us suffer.' But to keep a politician away from his convention is just like taking ice-cream away from a kid. It's liable to make 'em so mad there is not telling what they will pass." (May 25, 1932.)

But taking time off is something Congress can agree on.

"News of the day. Congress has promised the country that it will adjourn next Tuesday. Let's hope we can depend on it. If they do it will be the first promise they have kept this session. If they only hadn't promised it, there might be grounds for hope." (May 25, 1928.)

And sometimes they actually do what they say they will.

"Congress met and adjourned right away. One more day's salary for six hundred went up the taxpayers' flue. When do the taxpayers adjourn on pay?" (Dec. 6, 1926.)

"Don't ever tell us Friday is unlucky. Didn't Congress adjourn just today?

"The Republicans died fighting to keep from being investigated. The voters would like to investigate both parties as to their sanity the last few weeks. And there would be no hung jury as to their decision." (March 4, 1927.)

One more time:

"We sure had a great Fourth, especially after we picked up

our morning papers and found that Congress had adjourned the night of the third.

"That gave us a cause for having a fourth, but our enthusiasm was immediately dampened, for the Senate are to meet again Monday, so that means that prosperity will pick up only fifty per cent.

"This country has come to feel the same when Congress is in session as we do when the baby gets hold of a hammer. It's just a question of how much damage he can do with it before you can take it away from him. Well, in eighteen months these babies have left a record of devastation." (July 4, 1930.)

"The Republicans mopped up, the Democrats gummed up, and I will now try and sum up. Things are terribly dull now. We won't have any more serious comedy until Congress meets."

Chapter 4: Will Rogers the Man

Just who is this guy?

"Live your life so that whenever you lose, you're ahead."

William Penn Adair Rogers lived his life according to his own advice. He loved life, and he lived it to the fullest. He spent much of his life trying to make life more enjoyable for others.

(Quotes from Will Rogers in this book are taken from a variety of sources, notably the files of the Will Rogers Museum in Claremore, Okla. In this chapter particularly, however, most of the quotes are taken from the person who knew him best, his wife Betty, in her book *Will Rogers*, published in 1941 by the University of Oklahoma Press, Norman.)

Will was born Nov. 4, 1879, in what was then Indian Territory and is now Oklahoma. More specifically, he was born on a ranch he later called the Dog Iron Ranch near what later was known as the small town of Oologah, not far from Claremore in Northeast Oklahoma, in the distant shadow of Tulsa.

His dad, Clement Rogers ("Uncle Clem"), was one-fourth Cherokee Indian and a wealthy and prominent rancher at the time. His dad was a Confederate veteran of the Civil War, a Cherokee judge and a delegate to the Oklahoma Constitutional Convention. Rogers County, where Oologah and Claremore are located, was named after Clement Rogers (not Will Rogers).

Will was always proud of his Indian heritage. "My ancestors didn't come over on the Mayflower – they met the boat." His mother also was part Cherokee. Will sometimes claimed he was "one-eighth Cigar Store Indian."

Will was a good student and read a lot, but he never could generate a lot of interest in schooling. But he did take to ridin' and ropin' at an early age. "Like other Oklahoma kids, I was born bowlegged so I could set on a horse."

On reaching his teens he was a top cowhand, and already was doing rope tricks. His dad had expected him to move into the business circles, but Will was more interested in ridin' and ropin.' This attitude resulted in friction between Will and his dad, and undoubtedly was a factor in Will's wanderings away from home.

When it became obvious that Will did not much care for local schooling, he was sent first to a school in Neosho, and later to Kemper Military Academy, both in Missouri. Neither got much of his attention.

"There has always been some curiosity about how I left Kemper Military Academy – whether I jumped off or was I shoved," he said. "Well, I can't remember that far back."

So he left and went to work on ranches. Before long he switched to being a cowhand again, and eventually ended up in South America and later in South Africa.

You couldn't get much farther from the Oklahoma plains than a Wild West show in South Africa, but that could be considered the real start in Will Rogers's show business career. Up until that Wild West show, Will had been mostly a cowhand who could do amazing rope tricks.

An important part of his act, and probably one which set him apart from other trick ropers, was that he used his pony on the stage in his act in later years. This act eventually carried him to New Zealand and Australia, and later to Japan and China and then back to the United States.

One of the most important parts of his act came about by accident. During a matinee performance in Chicago, Will was doing one of his rope tricks when a dog from an animal act ran across the stage. Without thinking Will tossed his rope over the dog and caught it. The crowd erupted in applause.

"It gave me a tip," he said. "Instead of trying to keep on with a single roping act, I decided that people wanted to see me catch something."

He didn't just do "rope tricks." Some were amazing. One trick in particular landed him in the Guinness Book of Records, according to Joseph H. Carter, writing Will's biography for the Will Rogers Museum. In that trick Will threw three ropes at once. The first looped around the neck of a running horse, the second snared the rider on the horse and the third rope flipped under the horse and caught all four legs. His tricks were featured later in a movie, *"The Ropin' Fool."*

Will soon joined another Wild West show which was appearing at the World's Fair in St. Louis in 1904. The following year he performed his rope tricks at Madison Square Garden in New York City.

His ability to come up with a quip when something went wrong endeared him to audiences. On one occasion he was doing a trick which called for him to jump with both feet inside a spinning rope. It wasn't too hard to do, but this time he missed, getting just one foot in the rope. He turned it into a new trick: whenever he did this trick again, he missed on purpose. Then he would tell the crowd:

"Well, got all my feet through but one."

It was back in Oklahoma for a visit that another important factor in Will's life occurred. In Oologah he happened to run into a visiting young girl named Betty Blake. They didn't have too many visitors in tiny Oologah, but this lovely young lady from Arkansas was visiting her sister. She met Will, a gangling cowboy, and they soon fell in love. They were married in 1908. Will was 29 by then.

Another incident occurred which was a milestone in Will's career. Back in New York doing his rope tricks, one of those once-in-a-lifetime things suddenly popped up which helped launch Will as a wise-cracking, cowboy philosopher and humorist. One night a steer broke loose during a Wild West show, and as it was running into the crowd Will lassoed the animal and stopped any possible injuries. It wasn't too difficult for an expert roper like Will, but the New York newspapers turned him into a hero.

William Hammerstein of Broadway fame saw his act, and then signed him to a contract. Will began doing acts in New York theatrical stages and supper clubs, adding jokes and witty observations to his rope tricks. He was on the way.

It wasn't long before his audiences came to hear his folksy comments and jokes even more than watching his rope tricks. "He became recognized as being a very informed and smart philosopher – telling the truth in very simple words so that everyone could understand," as described by Joseph H. Carter.

One unusual thing about Will's performances was that he never repeated any of his jokes. He didn't keep using the same material – he commented on the news of the day, which of course changed every day, and tossed in whatever happened to pop into his head at the time. This eventually led to his appearances in the famous *Ziegfeld Follies*.

World War I was under way by then, and Will added his comments on international affairs to his regular philosophical observations and jokes. His fame was spreading.

Will was now appearing nightly on stage, and a lot of famous and important people came to listen to and laugh at his comments. He would still come on stage in his cowboy outfit, spinning rope tricks, and then make jokes about whatever news was grabbing the headlines that day.

He also began to make witty observations about some of the famous people who came to see him, along with prominent politicians of the day. His comments were never nasty, and the famous targets of his jokes laughed along with everyone else.

There was a subtle undertone to Will's jokes about the famous. He made fun of them, but he never embarrassed or ridiculed them.

He always talked about what was happening at the time, rather than recalling old jokes or experiences. He said he was not good at telling those old stories. "I never told a story in my life. What little humor I've got always pertains to now," he said.

His usual opening line, "All I know is what I read in the papers," became a household saying. And he was not just making that up – he did make jokes about what he read in the newspapers. Even his daily "Telegrams" frequently mentioned things he had just read in one of the newspapers he devoured each day.

But one time he learned that his jokes about current events fell flat unless his audience also kept up on the news in the papers. When he appeared before an audience of rich New York society women, they didn't understand his jokes about news events. Most of them did not read the papers.

"Then two nights later after that fiasco," Will said, "I went to Sing Sing and did a show for them and I never had as well a read audience in my life. They didn't miss a thing. Ever since then I have always felt we had the wrong bunch in there." (Sing Sing, of course, is a prison.)

With all of his appearances, Will was making a lot of money. But he never paid much attention to handling it. "Will had a haphazard way with money that was sometimes frightening," his wife Betty said in her book.

He never kept any financial records and sometimes didn't cash a paycheck for weeks. "Haven't got any bookkeeper or any bookkeeping," Will said. "We just put a check in the bank and draw on it until it's gone."

Over many years there have been a great many really funny comedians, comics, clowns, jokesters, team acts and, more recently, television entertainers. Will Rogers was consistently as funny as any of them and he also enjoyed one trait not shared by many – he wrote (or made up on the spot) all of his own stuff. He never relied on any professional or amateur funny men or women to help write his thousands of articles and columns, or create jokes for his stage shows.

By 1919 his name and funny comments had become household items of conversation. So he went to Hollywood and began making silent movies. He made a number of these movies, but returned to the stage in a few years. But about 1929 the movies became talkies, and Will returned to Hollywood and made 21 of the talkie movies. One of those movies, "State Fair" made in 1933, was being shown on a television channel as this was being written in 2012.

He enjoyed working in the movies. It was not nearly so hard as the frequent live stage performances. "It's the grandest show business I know anything about, and the only place where an actor can act and at the same time sit down in front and clap for himself."

While Will appeared in 48 silent movies, they were not the best way to display the Will Rogers wit. He became famous in part because of his Oklahoma cowboy way of tossing out jokes and funny comments. This was not possible in a movie with no sound. You couldn't hear him.

But when talkies appeared, Will Rogers found his place. He not only starred in a number of talkie movies, but he often ad-libbed and changed the scripts according to whatever leaped into his head at the moment. He appeared with many stars of the day, and his voice became immediately identifiable across the land.

No doubt he would have starred in television, if it had been developed in his time.

Like most stars, he was aware of his appearance. But unlike most, he did not constantly admire himself.

"Straight on I didn't look so good, and even sideways I wasn't so terrific, but a cross between a back and a three-quarters view, why, brother, I was hot. The way my ear (on the side) stood out from my head was just bordering on perfect. That rear view gave you just the shot needed. In those silent day pictures, that back right ear was a by-word from Coast to Coast."

He also tried to play down his own importance. He took it very hard when his sister, Maude, died. He wrote:

"Some uninformed newspapers printed: 'Mrs. C. L. Lane, sister of the famous comedian, Will Rogers.' It's the other way around. I am the brother of Mrs. C.L. Lane, the friend of humanity. And I want to tell you that, as I saw all those people who were there to pay tribute to her memory, it was the proudest moment of my life that I was her brother."

In the late 1920s Will also was heard on the radio from time to time. In 1930 he signed a contract for regular radio broadcasts, which featured his trademark observations, philosophy and jokes about current events and the world in general.

"They have a time getting me stopped on this radio thing," he told his listeners, "so I got an alarm clock here, and when it goes off, brother, I quit – even if I'm right in the middle of reciting 'Gunga Din' or "The Declaration of Independence.' I wouldn't need this alarm clock if I hadn't been so dumb about this broadcasting. You see, everybody reads everything they do over the radio and I'm going to learn it, but the trouble with me is I don't read very well and I hate to go to the trouble of writing this out. If I ever saw in print what I do say sometimes, I would be ashamed to say it."

It wasn't long after Will became famous as a humorist in New York City that he began writing his home-spun observations. This led to regular newspaper columns and the famous "Telegrams" which are quoted throughout this book. He also found time to write six books.

Will's writing is full of slang and words with strange spellings. He never paid much attention to grammar – and maybe he did that on purpose, to underscore his "cowboy approach." He might not have gone too far in formal schooling, but he was well educated by any meaningful standard.

In late 1922 Will began writing weekly articles, first in the *New York Times*, and later in papers across the nation. An article on Jan. 14, 1923, discussed an economic conference in Paris. In Will's view, it had about as much chance for success as similar conferences in 2012:

"England wants to settle one way with Germany, and France has a different plan. Now, as Germany owes both of them, there is no reason why each couldn't settle in their own way. But no, that's too easy. Nations don't do things that way. If they did, there would be no Diplomats, and Diplomats are nothing but high class Lawyers (some ain't even high class)."

Will's early writings were noticed by the so-called professional experts. Commented *The Nation*:

"His droll comments on men and events have become so

popular that he finds himself – probably to his surprise – a national figure. It is just as well for Mr. Rogers that his caustic observations are wrapped in humor. If they were delivered without the funny tags, his audience would set the dogs on him."

Added the *Saturday Review of Literature*:

"Somebody once gave him a license of free speech (or perhaps he took it without asking); but, at any rate, in the past few years he has probably turned over more heavy stones and thrown hot sunlight underneath than any man in the United States."

Not only did Will star on Broadway in New York, and appear in some 71 movies, both silent and talkie, but he also found time to get out and about. He traveled all over the world several times, taking a few moments out each day to crank out more than 4,000 newspaper columns. It has been estimated by various sources that Will wrote more than two million published words during his relatively short career.

That's a lot of cowboy philosophy and jokes, no matter how you measure it.

Sometimes he came up with a comment that, while not funny, was very thoughtful. Once, after he was famous, he was thinking of his early days. "Those were great old days, but darn it any old days are great old days. Even the tough ones, after they are over you can look back on them with great memories."

Speaking of cowboys, one of the most famous cowboys of them all credited Will Rogers for helping him get started in show business. Gene Autry, the famous fighting, singing cowboy, has told of how he was working as a night operator in Northeastern Oklahoma in 1927 when a man came in and wanted to send a telegram. It was Will Rogers.

Will stayed to talk with Gene, listened to him singing and playing and gave him a name to contact in New York.

In a tribute long after Will Rogers's death, Gene Autry wrote: "Humbly, and with a sense of deep affection and gratitude, I doff my Stetson to the greatest cowboy of them all – Will Rogers."

It seemed like Will never got tired. In addition to his stage appearances, movies and newspaper columns, he traveled back and forth across the United States – and later the world – appearing at all sorts of events as the featured speaker. He would joke and kid about some local interests at these appearances, but also bring up his comments about the famous.

He also never failed to stress good citizenship and democracy. He joked about how the government did things, or failed to do things, but he was serious about the welfare of Americans.

"America has a great habit of always talking about protecting American interests in some foreign country. Protect 'em here at home! There is more American interests right here than anywhere."

He also became a lecturer, traveling all across the nation. As his wife, Betty, reported, some of his most-quoted jokes were told at these lectures:

"I don't make jokes. I just watch the government and report the facts and I have never found it necessary to exaggerate." "The United States never lost a war or won a conference." "There is one thing a nation can't accuse us of – that is secret diplomacy. Our foreign dealings are an open book – generally a checkbook."

His schedule was frantic, but he found time to ride his beloved horses. A friend talked him into giving polo a try, and Will became an enthusiastic polo player.

"The people that think riding a horse is all there is to polo are the same people who think that anybody that can walk makes a good golfer, or anybody who looks good in a bathing suit would make a good swimmer," he said.

He also found out quickly that a rider can get bruised if not really hurt: "The people who watched us play our Sunday games soon learned that in a spill, if the falling rider hit on his feet, it was Fred Stone. If he hit on his head, it was me. We were both equally safe."

He had an eventful game once in a polo tournament:

"Things were going along pretty good until along about the third chukker. I was on a new pony that suddenly reared up and fell back on me. There he was lying right across my intermission. My head was out on one side and my feet on the other. That was all you could see. Next day in another game I'm on my horse, coming lickety-split down the field, when for no reason at all the horse crossed his front legs and starts turning somersaults. They picked me up just south of Santa Barbara. The crowd all said, 'Oh, that's Will Rogers; he just does that for laughs.'"

Many of his special appearances were at fund-raisers. He helped raise money for victims of floods, earthquakes and other disasters.

With all his comments on current events it was inevitable that politics would attract the attention of Will Rogers. Government bungling and inefficiency, in fact, became favorite targets. The U.S. Senate soon climbed to the top of his jibes.

Will himself was a Democrat, but he needled politicians of any party. He pooh-poohed any notion of him becoming a candidate for anything, but he did agree to serve as a good-will ambassador to Mexico on one occasion, and also became mayor of Beverly Hills for a brief period.

"They say I'll be a comedy mayor. Well, I won't be the only one. I never saw a mayor yet that wasn't comical. As to my administration, I won't say I'll be exactly honest, but I'll agree to split 50-50 with you and give the town an even break. I'm for the common people, and as Beverly Hills has no common people, I'll be sure to make good."

Presidential campaigns were a favorite whipping boy for Will Rogers. He thought the campaigns were stupid and a waste of time. To emphasize his point, in 1928 he ran for president as the candidate of the Anti-Bunk Party. His only promise to the voters was that, if elected, he would resign. On election day he announced that he had won, and promptly fulfilled his promise: he resigned.

At the Democratic nominating convention in 1924, he wrote about the first week:

"I wish you could have been here and heard what great men we have in this country. We started out with 16 men for president. Here is what each one of them was – 'The only man who can carry the Democratic party to a glorious victory in November. Whose every act has been an inspiration to his fellow men. Not only loved in his Home State but in every State.' We have had six continuous days of 'The Man I am about to name to you.' And you could never tell until one got through who he was going to name. They all kept the names until the last word. It was safer. One guy from Montana, Maloney, was the hit of the convention. He forgot his speech and didn't say anything. They applauded for five minutes."

Will joked about a lot of U.S. presidents, but he was always careful to keep it light and easy. At one appearance in 1916, it was the first time a president actually attended the show. President Woodrow Wilson and his wife unexpectedly showed up. Will was very nervous.

"Finally a warden knocked on my dressing-room door and said, 'You die in five more minutes for kidding your country.' They just literally shoved me out on the stage."

Will at first admitted to the crowd that "I'm kinder nervous here tonight," but went on with his act. Then he warmed up and began tossing out his jokes.

"Everybody in the house, before they would laugh, looked at the president to see how he was going to take it. Well, he started laughing and they all followed suit."

Anyone was fair game for Will's needling, but he did not get carried away with his jokes. "You can always kid a big man," he said. "I generally hit the fellow on top because it's not fair to hit a man when he's down."

When he met President Harding, Will said the president repeated some jokes that Will had just told about him at a show.

"No, I don't think I ever hurt any man's feelings by my little gags," Will once said. "I know I never willfully did it. I may not have always said just what they would have liked me to say, but they knew it was meant in good nature and in fun."

But once he almost went too far. During a talk on the radio, he told listeners that he had a friend there who wanted to speak to them. Then he imitated the high-pitched voice of President Coolidge and said:

"Ladies and Gentleman, I am supposed to deliver a message every year on the condition of the country. I find the Country as a WHOLE prosperous. I don't mean by that, that the WHOLE country is prosperous, But as a WHOLE, its prosperous, That is its prosperous as a WHOLE, a WHOLE is not supposed to be prosperous, There is not a WHOLE lot of doubt about that."

A lot of listeners thought the speaker was really Coolidge. Will worried about it, but President Coolidge sent him a personal note, saying he knew it was in fun.

Will maintained the Rogers family ranch and house near Oologah, and also had a ranch in California. He bought the

California ranch when he was traveling that way to make movies. He never gave up his love for horses and roping. He practiced his roping at both ranches, and played polo at his California ranch.

Although he was a welcome and familiar figure at the homes and palaces of famous and important people all over the world, he considered himself just a home-lovin' cowboy. He and his wife Betty were the parents of four children. Their youngest son died at the age of two from diphtheria. He taught the others to ride and love horses.

While horses were a deep love for Will Rogers, it wasn't long before flying became a close second. He flew anywhere whenever he got the chance, and became an outspoken advocate for flying in America.

Among his flying friends was Charles Lindbergh, who was the first to fly solo across the Atlantic. Will often hitchhiked on airmail planes in the early days before commercial flights were available.

Will told of one occasion he flew with Lindbergh when they landed at a rough field:

"Lindbergh said he was going to land at a field where there was no hangar – nothing to show which way the wind was blowing. 'How can you tell how to land when you don't know which way the wind is blowing?' I said to him. And he says, 'Why, didn't you see the way those clothes were blowing on that line a while ago?' I hadn't even noticed the clothes, so I said, 'Well, suppose it wasn't Monday, what would you do then? I guess we'd have to fly around till they washed, is that it?' Say, listen, I wasn't kidding this boy. He come right back at me. He said, 'I wouldn't fly over such a dirty country.'"

Will never passed up a chance to promote aviation. One of his close friends was General Billy Mitchell, a pioneer Army Aviation officer. Will would tell anyone who would listen that aviation would become a key factor in our military some day.

Airplane crashes were not rare in those days, and Will survived several of them – two on one day in different aircraft.

Ironically, he died at the early age of 55 when a small plane crashed on Aug. 15, 1935, in the remote, far north part of Alaska. The pilot was Wiley Post, a fellow Oklahoman and famous pilot who wore a patch over one eye. Will flew often with Wiley. They were on the first leg of another of Will's trips to different parts of the world when the plane crashed.

* * * *

Will continued his daily "Telegrams" from wherever he happened to be at the moment. His last few words, written the very morning of his fatal crash, were sent from Fairbanks, Alaska, on Aug. 15, 1935. At that time Alaska was still a territory, and had not yet become a state. Here is Will's last dispatch, which came after a visit to a nearby New Deal farming colony started that May to settle and develop Alaska:

"Visited our new emigrants. Now this is no time to discuss whether it will succeed or whether it won't, whether it's farming country or whether it is not, and to enumerate the hundreds of mistakes and confusions and rows and arguments and management in the whole thing at home and here.

"As I see it, there is now but one problem now that they are here, that's to get 'em housed within six or eight weeks. Things have been a terrible mess. They are getting 'em straightened out, but even now not fast enough. There is about 700 or 800 of 'em. About 200 went back; also about that many workmen sent from the transient camps down home (not CCC) and just lately they are using about 150 Alaska workmen paid regular wages. But it's just a few weeks to snow now and they have to be out of the tents, both workers and settlers.

"Plenty food and always has been and will be. They can always get that in, but it's houses they need right now and Colonel Hunt in charge realizes it.

"You know after all there is a lot of difference in pioneering for gold and pioneering for spinach.

"Yours, WR"

Chapter 5: Democrats and Republicans

It's just a big party

"I used to try to get what I thought would be some funny political angles over the radio, and it was awful hard.

"But last night along came my old friend Nick Longworth on the air and hit on a humorous angle that I had never thought of, and I bet none of you had either. He blamed the Democratic party for the financial depression that is enveloping the world.

"It's really the biggest advertisement that the Democratic party have ever had. Why, if they was that important, they wouldn't be Democrats. They would all be Republicans, but it was a new reason at that.

"Did you ever notice, that there has never been a year when alibis were as scarce?" (Oct. 7, 1930.)

When things are normal, which definitely does not describe 2011 and 2012, you will find the Democrats and Republicans criticizing each other, arguing and sometimes even getting a little hostile. This is especially true in an election year, which 2012 happens to be.

Things are getting hostile all right, and often downright nasty. But so far it's not the Democrats and Republicans. This time the Republicans are fighting each other.

In particular, Newt Gingrich, a former speaker of the U.S. House of Representatives and a veteran Washington insider if there ever was one, alternately looked like the best candidate in decades and in the next moment he appeared and sounded like some television stooge.

Newt, with all his admirable qualities, sometimes personified that old "put his foot in his mouth again" politician.

"In the hours after Newt Gingrich emerged as the latest front runner in the Republican presidential race, he began to refer to himself as "Newt Gingrich" in an interview with Sean Hannity. He also began to employ the royal "we," as in "We would have about two hours after the Inaugural Address, we would stop and sign between 200 Executive Orders and presidential findings.".
. – Joe Klein in Time magazine, Dec. 19, 2011.

But not everyone saw Newt as the Republican savior and new hope.

"Republican insiders are rising up to cut Newt Gingrich down to size, testament to the GOP establishment's fear that the mercurial candidate could lead the party to disaster this fall."
-- Charles Babington of the Associated Press in the St. Joseph News-Press, Jan. 28, 2012.

Will Rogers also took a long look at the Republicans.

"The Republicans have had a saying for some time, 'The Roosevelt honeymoon is over.'

"They were mighty poor judges of a love-sick couple. Why he and the people have got a real love match, and it looks like it would run for at least six years.

"If there is one thing the Republican party has got to learn it is that you can't get votes by just denouncing. You got to offer some plan of your own. They only had one problem, 'Elect us, and maybe we can think of something to do after we get in, but up to now we haven't thought of it, but give us a chance, we may.'" (Nov. 7, 1934.)

President Obama could not resist pouring a little fuel on the fire.

Referring to Obama's State of the Union speech and his

references to Republicans, Joe Klein in the Time issue of Feb. 6, 2012, wrote:

"It seemed he had learned something from watching Gingrich's debate performances. The blunt power of the central declaration of the speech. . . was the sort of line Gingrich has used time and time again to excoriate journalists, except Obama delivered it better, without the sneer."

Despite all the ridiculous claims in political speeches, many "experts" maintain that jobs and the economy are the things that concern voters.

Will agreed:

"See what happened in England. No matter what government or party is in, if you have your election during the hard times they will throw 'em out on their ears. The Republicans have just from now till Summer to make things look better or out in the alley they go." (Oct. 28, 1931.)

But, Will says, have hope:

"Be a Republican and sooner or later you will be a Postmaster."

Early 2012 is the time for candidates for president. Obama has the Democratic nomination sewed up, of course, since he is already in the White House. In years past, just as today, others looked longingly toward the White House:

"Today I read where a speech that Franklin D. Roosevelt had made just about threw him in the ring as the next Democratic candidate.

"Now there is a fine man. In fact, that is one of the characteristics of the Democratic party, that they have had some of the finest men as candidates that we have in this country, and it's almost a shame that they are to be eternally handicapped by being 'right but never president.'

"But you can start now by trying to dig up something and in three years you won't have found anything wrong with Franklin D. Roosevelt outside of being a Democrat." (July 7, 1929.)

Sometimes it would seem that it is unnecessary to have an election to pick a president. There are plenty of "political experts" and polls to tell us exactly what is going to happen. The fact that they are often wrong doesn't slow them down a bit. This also is nothing new.

"I have read New Year's predictions till I am blue in the face about the great future of Stay-Froze Ice Chest, chewing gum, hot water bottles, Mme. Ginsberg's face cream, reducing belts, and one-man machine guns, but I have yet to see one word on what 1930 holds in store for the Democrats. And that's the very thing that makes me believe us Democrats may get a break in the coming year. I base my faith on the fact that 98 per cent of all predictions are wrong, and on the fact that it's an off-year in politics and all off years are Democratic years." (Dec. 31, 1929.)

You would think that after so many years of political battling, the major parties would come up with some new tactics. But they seem to get in a rut and stay there.

"Politics pretty quiet over the weekend. Democrats are attacking and Republicans defending. All the Democrats have to do is promise 'what they would do if they got in.' But the Republicans have to promise 'what they would do' and then explain why they haven't already 'done it.'

"I do honestly believe the Republicans have reformed and want to do better. But whether they have done it in time to win the election is another thing. The old voter is getting so he wants to be saved before October every election year." (Sept. 26, 1932.)

If we can just suffer through all this early political wrangling and backbiting, we can always look forward to the summer of 2012 (and every four years afterward) for the political conventions. These are the times when major decisions are made on the political candidates. The conventions are a sort of major circus.

"Well here I am right at the stage door waiting to see all the actors in this great comedy called 'a convention field for no reason at all.'

"I have the distinction of being the first Democrat white child to arrive at the Republican fiasco. Breakfast at home Saturday morning, dinner in Kansas City, then into Chicago for breakfast Sunday, but disgraced myself by making the last hop on the train, as there was no regular plane. Guess I am getting old, going back, be taking up golf next.

"A newspaper man spoiled my whole convention by asking me if 'I was an alternate.' Now a delegate is bad enough, but an alternate is just a spare tire for a delegate. An alternate is the lowest form of political life there is. He is the parachute in the plane that never leaves the ground." (June 12, 1932.)

Those strange people who get involved in political campaigns make up all sorts of crazy stuff against other candidates. There ought to be a law against tactics like that.

"Poor Democrats. I love 'em. I guess it's because some are so dumb. Now they are dying to scare up an issue by trying to discredit Mr. Hoover, because some lobbyist wrote a letter saying that he knew President Hoover's secretary, and that the secretary was very partial to Cuban sugar in his coffee in the morning, and that in view of this dastardly plot Mr. Hoover should really be impeached. Then they wonder whey they don't get anywhere." (Dec. 23, 1929.)

Meanwhile, the campaigning goes on and on. And on and on.

"Well, I see where Mr. Roosevelt in New Jersey had a big Democratic rally and mosquito rodeo.

"There was 100 Democrats there applauding, or fighting mosquitoes, you couldn't tell which. A few Republicans were there to cheer the insects on in their good work.

"The original Roosevelt used to call it 'pussyfooting.' This one took in the whole cat. He called it 'pussycatting.'" (Aug. 28, 1932.)

It takes money to run a campaign, lots of money. All sorts of methods are tried to raise funds.

"I been hearing appeals over the radio for funds and I thought sure it must be for Florida or Porto Rico or some equally deserving cause and come to find out it was the Democratic campaign treasurer seeking first aid.

"Nights when the candidates don't talk over the radio, why their treasurers do, asking for money enough to pay for the radio for the next night for the candidate. Both parties have got to a point now where they will take old clothes or second-hand cars, or anything.

"There is peculiar charities in this country." (Oct. 5, 1928.)

Despite all the babble and arm-waving, all the campaigning usually comes down to the same old things.

"Talk about economizing and cutting out all unnecessarys, what's the idea of holding the Chicago Republican convention?

"This morning's papers announced Mr. Hoover's campaign plan, the route, the towns, who he would shake hands with, and what he would wear.

"As for the platform, it will be the same one they have read for forty years but never had.

"And the speeches will be the same ones delivered for forty years but never listened to." (April 20, 1932.)

And of course the conventions usually boil down to the same old routines.

"I am here in Clem Shaver's, the head of the Democrats, home town. He tells me that the Democrats are going to be so peaceful and hungry for harmony at their convention that you won't hardly know they are Democrats.

"Well, if I go there and they are as he says, I will ask for my money back. They have worked for years to bring their conventions up to a show and now they want to crab it." (April 20, 1928.)

Ah, but the speeches. You can't have politicians without speeches, and you sure can't have political conventions without all sorts of speeches.

"See by this morning's paper where Al Smith is going to make sixteen speeches, all different.

"Now off-hand, that looks like a pretty hard thing to do, but it's not. You could put sixteen different interpretations on the Democratic platform and still not exhaust half the alibis. And Hoover could speak incessantly on that Republican promissory note.

"If I was a politician I would pick out one good reason and one good speech and stay with it. Lindbergh only made one speech all over America, and is a hero yet. But if a politician was that smart he wouldn't be a politician." (July 2, 1928.)

On a trip across the Pacific on a ship, Will Rogers contemplated the politicians.

"I just found out who China is like. It's the Democrats at home. Individually they are smart, likeable and efficient, but let two get together and they both want to be president.

"Formed a new government at Nanking yesterday and nobody would let the other be head man, so they called it a committee government. Now everybody is president.

"There's a new idea for you Democrats." (Jan. 3, 1932.)

Will, who was a self-proclaimed Democrat, made a lot of jokes at the Democrats' expense. But he did not ignore the Republicans.

"Smith in Sedalia, Mo., read some figures and records of Republican economy. The Department of Agriculture had spent $45,000,000 more in '27 than in '24. That means that cost of 'promise of relief' has advanced that much. Mellon's department had saved some money, but it cost fifty million more to save it than it did the same department in '24, showing that even the cost of saving money is going up.

"They have also been printing government documents on both sides of the paper. I don't know how anyone ever found it out that they were using both sides." (Oct. 17, 1928.)

Sometimes Will's looks at things took on a rather unusual twist.

"In a Sunday article I stated that the Donner Party was our only cannibalism. I was wrong, as usual, for I just learned of this case.

"Crossing the divide from Utah to Colorado in 1872 a man named Packard evidently practiced it. He was convicted in Del Norte, Colo., and the judge passed sentence as follows:

"'Packard, you have committed the world's most fiendish crime. You not only murdered your companions, but you ate up every Democrat in Hillsdale County. You are to hang by the neck till you are dead, and may God have mercy on your Republican soul.'

"They lived off the Democrats, but this was only one we could ever convict." (Oct. 12, 1930.)

Will did not back off from mentioning the women, either.

"Here is a funny situation. The women anti-prohibitionists

said, 'We will support the party that comes out for direct appeal.'

"And they would if it had been the Republican party. But, as luck would have it, it was those 'mangy' Democrats instead.

"Now, most of these women are wealthy Republicans. And they are having a time now trying to get out of it.

"The ladies want prohibition repealed all right, but not bad enough to repeal the Republican party with it. They want it wet, but not wet enough to be Democratic

"In other words, politics is thicker than beer." (July 13, 1932.)

Chapter 6: U.S. Senate

When in doubt, filibuster. . .

"Diary of a United States Senate trying to find $2,000,000,000 that they have already spent but didn't have.

"Monday – Soak the rich.

"Tuesday – Begin hearing from the rich.

"Tuesday afternoon – Decide to give the rich a chance to get richer.

"Wednesday – Tax Wall Street stock sales.

"Thursday – Get word from Wall Street, 'Lay off us or you will get no campaign contributions.'

"So Thursday afternoon – Decide 'We was wrong about Wall Street.'

"Friday – Soak the little fellow.

"Saturday morning – Find out there is no little fellow. He has been soaked till he is drowned.

"Sunday – Meditate.

"Next week – Same procedure, only more talk and less results." (May 8, 1932.)

You sort of get the idea, after reading the comments of Will Rogers, that he didn't think the U.S. Senate accomplished very much. You get that same idea yourself after you discover how little the Senate has accomplished lately.

"Funny thing, in the same paper Saturday that told about the Senate vs. Honesty, the Coolidge auto-biography in that very day's installment said: 'If the Senate has weakness it's because the people send men lacking in ability and character, but that is not the fault of the Senate, it can't choose its members. It has to work with what is sent to it. When I was elected vice president I was going to learn the rules of the Senate, then I found out that the Senate had but one rule and that was that the Senate would do anything it wanted to do whenever it wanted to do it.'

"Now there's the words of a man that listened to 'em for two years and argued with 'em for six." (Feb. 5, 1933.)

It might be a good thing if American voters paid attention to former President Calvin Coolidge. As noted above, you can't blame the U.S. Senate for accomplishing little, if you elect people to serve in the Senate who can't or won't do anything.

But sometimes the Senate is good for a laugh:

"Not only the week's biggest laugh but the year's biggest guffaw come from the United States Senate during the oil lobby hearing. They discovered that Senators were trading oil votes for sugar votes. They were surprised and practically dumbfounded that such a condition could exist. Yes, just about as surprising to everybody that knows politics as it would be to discover that Herbert Hoover was born in the United States, was over 30 years old and white.

"Vote trading got 'em all in the Senate and kept them in there (if the trades were good enough).

"A Senator learns to 'swap' at the same age a calf learns which end of his mother is the dining room." (March 2, 1930.)

Will Rogers proposed an amendment of his own after the Senate finally passed something:

"After one more day of useless argument, in a useless session, the Senate has passed the Naval Treaty. I wanted to get this amendment in, and I believe if it had been put to a vote of the people it would have gone in:

"'We sign this treaty because we sent a fine delegation over and they did the best they could, and we will back 'em up, but this is the last one we will sign.

"'While the whole idea sounds fine, it's a lot of hooey in practice. You can no more tell a nation which gun he is to shoot you with than you can tell him what he is to wear while shooting you.

"'So, we hereby plead with all nations, let's quit holding conferences, stop conferring and just be friends again.'" (July 21, 1930.)

But even the U.S. Senate has to agree that sometimes things are tough.

"The whole country, including Nicholas Murray Butler, been knocking the Senate so much lately till they just had a session yesterday and held a clinic over their own body.

"And, do you know they couldn't find a thing wrong with themselves. Both parties just spent the session scratching each other's back, and us paying for the manicure.

"But give the devil his due. They have had their troubles. Every time they went to tax something a voter would rise up and say, 'Yeah?'

"It's been a tough year to be a Senator. It's been a tough year to be anything. Even Capone has a tough year, so what can you expect from other industries?" (May 24, 1932.)

Unlike the U.S. Senate in 2012, one Senate in Will's time actually paid a little attention to the president. Of course, that doesn't mean they agreed with him.

"The Senate just sits and waits till they find out what the president wants so they know how to vote against him.

"Be a good joke on 'em if he didn't let them know, or for instance, if he had announced that he was going to let the Wickersham committee go and didn't want any more money voted for 'em, why they would have voted them a million dollars.

"That's the way Mr. Coolidge used to do. He would keep 'em guessing so long as they voted his way accidentally part of the time." (June 29, 1930.)

Even though he kidded them a lot, Will Rogers actually liked most of the senators he knew. When he said "I never met a man I didn't like," he must have included U.S. senators.

"I like to make jokes and kid about the senators. They are a never-ending source of amusement, amazement and discouragement. But the rascals, when you meet 'em they are mighty nice fellows. It must be something in the office that makes them so ornery sometimes. When you see what they do official, you want to shoot 'em. But when he looks at you and grins so innocently, you kinder want to kiss him." ("Will Says.")

"There is no race of people in the world that can compete with a senator for talking. If I went to the Senate, I couldn't talk fast enough to answer roll call."

"About being a U.S. Senator, the only thing the law says you have to be is 30 years old. Not another single requirement. They just figure that a man that old got nobody to blame but himself if he gets caught there."

"It won't be no time until some woman will become so desperate politically and lose all prospectus of right and wrong and maybe go from bad to worse and finally wind up in the Senate. Men gave 'em the right to vote but never meant for them to take it seriously. But being women they took the wrong meaning and did."

Will had long encouraged the Congress to adopt a policy where they would not appropriate money for something without stating where the money should come from.

Now and then some senator or representative will try to get something along that line accomplished, but usually gets nowhere. It was true in 1933, and it's still true in 2012.

"A senator named Tydings the other day introduced a bill where the government couldn't appropriate more money than was coming in. That is, if you didn't have any money you could not dole out any.

"Well the Senate like to mobbed him. They called the idea treason, sacreligious, inhuman and taking the last vestige of power for a politician, that is, the right to appropriate your money which you don't have." (Jan. 29, 1933.)

Maybe the Senate doesn't do too well when it comes to handling money, but no one can doubt them when it comes to talking.

"At Las Vegas, Nevada, Secretary Wilbur is dedicating the Boulder Dam. I had been asked to be there in case Arizona Senators should start a filibuster and keep talking and talking to prevent the dedication.

"They wired, 'Will, you are the only man in America that can talk longer about nothing, than a Senator. Then, too, we think the Democratic party should be represented and Borah can't come.'" (Sept. 17, 1930.)

It's not often that a Senator has nothing to say.

"Col. T. Coleman Du Pont, United States Senator from Delaware, has lost use of his vocal cords. Now I feel sincerely sorry for his personal discomfiture, but if his ailment could be made contagious and he distribute it among his brother members of the Senate his illness would prove to be a tremendous national blessing.

"Since Senator Fess has been reprimanded for complimenting Coolidge, and Magruder has Philadephia sunk from under him,

I have been accused of being lax in my national criticism for fear of exile. I want to say that I am only trying to think up something terrible enough to say." (Oct. 28, 1927.)

Sometimes Will Rogers went to the scene of the discussion to see for himself what was going on.

"Senator Brookhart has just been down at Panama and he was shocked and said the people down here were 'just wallowing in sin,' and he was going to introduce a bill in Congress to remove the canal to go between Cedar Rapids and Des Moines. So the people here asked me to come down to offset Brookhart and I kinder wanted to see (and perhaps join the wallowing).

"I will say this for the folks down here. They are not wallowing in the canal. I flew in here yesterday from Costa Rica and I haven't seen the canal yet and can't find anybody that knows where it is.

"There is one great thing about the tropics – it gives you a great alibi." (April 12, 1931.)

A key part of American government is the so-called separation of powers, which loosely means that the executive branch (the president), the legislative (Congress) and the judicial (Supreme Court) are each separate from the others and sort of act as a check on the others. Good theory, but it doesn't always work too well. The Founding Fathers probably didn't figure that there would be a lot of infighting, and hoped they would work with each other.

"Mr. Hoover is becoming a typical American president by becoming disgusted with the Senate early in his administration.

"Distrust of the Senate by presidents started with Washington, who wanted to have 'em court-martialed. Jefferson proposed life imprisonment for 'em, old Andy Jackson said, 'To hell with 'em,' and got his wish. Lincoln said the Lord must have hated 'em, for he made so few of 'em.

"Roosevelt whittled a big stick and beat on 'em for six years.

Taft just laughed at them and grew fat. They drove Wilson to an early grave. Coolidge never let 'em know what he wanted, so they never knew how to vote against him, and Mr. Hoover took 'em serious, thereby making his only political mistake." (Nov. 1, 1929.)

Sometimes even a senator loses patience with others in the Senate.

"It sure did kick up some excitement in the Senate when Senator Moses called the other senators 'sons of wild jackasses.' Well, if you think it made the senators hot, you wait till you see what happens when the jackasses hear how they have been slandered.

"This Moses, like the one in the original cast, is a kind of amateur prophet, and every once in a while he climbs to the top of some speaker's table, strikes the stone head of a toastmaster and brings forth a wisecrack. So next week I can see the Senate passing a resolution to have his form again enveloped in some distant bulrushes." (Nov. 10, 1929.)

"Confucius perspired out more knowledge than the U.S. Senate has vocalized out in the last 50 years." ("Will Says.")

But even if they don't always get along, sometimes a senator will seek a president's help.

"Senator Reed Smoot interrupted President Hoover's weekend vacation in Virginia with a plea to please help the sugar industry. There is 120,000,000 of us eat it, and exactly 1,231 that raise it. But Reed has dedicated his entire political career to make sugar not only sweet but dear to the 120,000,000.

"Lot's wife (or somebody in the Bible) turned around to look back and turned into salt. If Reed ever glances back we are going to have a human sugar bowl on our hands." (Aug. 4, 1929.)

Since 2012 is an election year, there will be some new senators to be sworn in for the next session (beginning in early 2013). There are some critics who are hoping the entire Senate will be new members, but of course that won't happen. (If for no other reason, all members are not up for reelection this year.)

"Say, with all this argument we have had about what Mr. Taft said when he swore in President Hoover, why not bring out what Vice President Curtis said when he swore in the first six senators? (You know we got 'em in half dozen lots, just like eggs.) Instead of saying 'with no mental reservations' he got his English and his Kaw mixed and really said 'with no mental obligations.'

"Being in the Senate as long as he has and seeing the type, why the chances are that he was honest with this government and swore 'em in that way purposely. After all it don't make much difference to the country how they get in there. How to get 'em out, that's our problem." (March 20, 1929.)

Maybe it's not intentional, but sometimes the Senate can be a little funny.

"The biggest laugh of the week was caused, naturally, by a senator (and they wasn't even in session, not even trying to be funny).

"It was by Jim Watson of Indiana, the Republican leader. The 'Progressives' are holding a meeting in Washington and he asked them to please define exactly how they stood on the following problems.

"Asking the Progressives to answer something that a Republican wouldn't answer if he was on his death-bed!" (March 11, 1931.)

Did you ever try to call a senator or one of your representatives on the telephone?

"We finally got the real low-down on the intelligence of the Senate. The Capitol building put in dial telephones and out of ninety-six members only two knew enough to work 'em. And both those members were men who had been defeated at the last election, showing they knew entirely too much to be in there.

"So they are going to have them taken out. There is nobody to put the blame on but yourself if you get the wrong number. They want nothing connected with the Senate in any way where the responsibility can't be shifted.

"P.S. Los Angeles census is not out yet. Our surveyors are still annexing more territory. We had Mexico City, and the League of Nations made us give it back." (May 23, 1930.)

"The United States Senate opens with a prayer and closes with an investigation." ("Will Says.")

Just the facts. The Senate wants all the facts.

"The Senate committee demanding every little confidential paper exchanged between Mr. Hoover and Ramsay MacDonald (in supposed confidence) is just like a couple producing their marriage certificate in court, and then being made to go back and produce all the love letters they wrote to each other during the courtship.

"Mr. Hoover ought to be like the Bishop. Tell 'em it's none of their business.

"But the Senate is not as scared of the president as they are the Bishop. The president don't control the Methodist vote.

"What does the Senate do with all the knowledge they demand from other people? They never seem to use it." (June 12, 1930.)

A senator pays a visit to Will.

"Senator Shipstead of Minnesota paid me a little visit at the ranch Sunday. He ain't either a Democrat or Republican, and it was mighty refreshing to talk to somebody who could tell you the truth about both sides. He is the only senator who don't have to have a convention to tell him what to think." (Oct. 28, 1930.)

Even the U.S. Senate has to take time off now and then.

"The Senate adjourned and this is what happened in twelve hours:

"Weather turned cool.

"Market picked up.

"Fish started biting.

` "Man 97 years old whipped his son 57 for using profanity.

"Girl posing as Indian princess (and by the way there is no such thing as an American Indian princess) well, she said she was a parachute jumper. Got up there, got scared to jump and the pilot kicked her out. I nominate him for the Nobel prize.

"Marconi father of a baby.

"Hunter boys, endurance fliers, arrived here. They laid over in Riverside, sixty miles away, last night to rest up for the trip in." (July 22, 1930.)

Chapter 7: Economy and Business

Business is the backbone. . .

"Say, it's costing me money to keep you all informed. I had to read so much about this word 'debenture,' and nobody here in Boston couldn't tell me what it meant. I had to go buy a dictionary. I knew before I looked it up that it was some camouflaged word that wouldn't do the farmers any good.

"'Debenture, a certificate serving as a voucher for a debt.'

"That ain't nothing but just a plain old note, giving and taking, and going on friends' 'debentures' is what makes the farmer need relief. Besides, it's the middleman that don't raise the wheat but just ships it. He is the one that gets the 'debenture.' That ain't farm relief. That bill ought to be called exporters' relief bill." (April 22, 1929.)

One of the biggest problems facing the nation as we approach the November presidential election in 2012 is the federal debt. President Clinton managed to run up some surplus funds, and hoped they would be applied to the debt. But under Republican President Bush – who had a war to fight – and Democratic President Obama the federal debt has soared into more trillions.

It is difficult for the little guy to understand just how much a trillion dollars is. (The big guys don't seem to understand either. And the politicians keep spending it, when they don't have it.)

"The point is to note that what happened to us did not drop from the mesosphere. It was manufactured by a political process running on myths, lies and the purchase of political influence by moneyed interests." -- Froma Harrop of Creators Syndicate, published in Oct. 31, 2011, St. Joseph News-Press.

The rich get richer and the poor get poorer: "There is one rule that works in every calamity. Be it pestilence, war or famine, the rich get richer and poor get poorer. The poor even help arrange it." ("Will Says.")

"The difference between our rich and poor grows greater every year. Our distribution of wealth is getting more uneven all the time. A man can make a million and he is on every page in the morning. But it never tells you who gave up that million he got. You can't get money without taking it from somebody." ("Will Says.")

There are plenty of financial experts who will tell us what went wrong. There are plenty of political "experts" who will tell us they know how to fix everything. Oh?

"Why don't somebody print the truth about our present economic situation? We spent six years of wild buying on credit (everything under the sun, whether we needed it or not) and now we are having to pay for 'em under Mr. Hoover, and we are howling like a pet coon.

"P.S. – This would be a great world to dance in if we didn't have to pay the fiddler." (June 27, 1930.)

The United States has gone through tough economic times before, of course, and inevitably the doomsayers screamed that the end of everything was just over the next hill. But somehow, we managed to stagger through. Some more responsible and thoughtful observers usually pointed out that these economic cycles always came around sooner or later. And, sooner or later, things would get better.

Meanwhile, in 2011 and 2012, it sometimes seemed as if the doomsayers this time just might be right.

"The ranks of America's poorest poor have climbed to a record high – 1 in 15 people – spread widely across metropolitan areas as the housing bust pushed many inner-city poor into suburbs and other outlying places and shriveled jobs and income." -- Hope Yen and Laura Wides-Munoz of the Associated Press, in the Nov. 3, 2011, St. Joseph News-Press.

Well, it's not the first time.

"This country is so hungry this morning they could eat a lame duck.

"If you want to really know one of the major things that's wrong with us, go take a nickel and get last week's Saturday Evening Post and read the first article in there. It's by Sam Blythe. Then go out, and before you buy the baby a rattle, your sweetheart a tooth brush, your wife a pair of rubber boots, ask if they were 'made in America.'

"Then you can show your patriotism, and not just keep saying 'What's the matter with this country?'

"England is doing it; the world is doing it. But our society don't think they smell right unless they been dipped in foreign perfume." (Dec. 6, 1932.)

In other words, charity begins at home. It was true 80 years ago in 1932, and it's true in 2012. America should buy American products.

"America can carry herself and get along in pretty fair shape, but when she stops and picks up the whole world and puts it on her shoulders she just can't 'get it done.'" ("Will Says.")

According to a genuine financial expert (Will Rogers; he makes more sense than those self-proclaimed geniuses), it's crazy to spend money we don't have. Congress is the best example of that, of course, but one look at the money owed on credit cards today will convince anyone that lots of people also spend money they don't have yet. Our expert, Will Rogers, also urges that we try to save a little money now and then.

"Everybody is saying that the trouble with the country is that people are saving instead of spending. Well, if that's a vice then I am Einstein. Since when did saving become a national calamity?

"I know it's terrible for a nonauthority like me to tell you to go contrary to expert advice, but I am telling you if you got a dollar soak it away, put it in a savings bank, bury it, do anything but spend it.

"Spending when we didn't have it puts us where we are today. Saving when we got it will get us back to where we was before we went cuckoo." (Nov. 24, 1930.)

Buying things when you don't have the money usually works out to being in debt, at least for a while.

"About all that was in the papers this morning was about 'debts.' Every nation, and every individual, their principal worry is 'debt.'

"What would be the matter with this for relieving practically everybody's 'depression' – just call all debts off?

"There can't be over a dozen men in the world that are owed more than they owe, so you wouldn't be hurting very many and besides if you do give them some worry, that's what they had everybody else doing for years.

"It's not supply and demand, it's old man interest that's got the world by the ears.

"This would give great temporary relief to 99 per cent and wouldn't hurt the others long for they soon would have it back again.

"I make a motion. Do I hear a second?" (June 7, 1931.)

It happens to every columnist and every comedian. Sooner

or later someone will challenge something the columnist or comedian wrote or said. Will Rogers was no exception.

"Got some news for you. Fellow wrote the New York Times (my mother paper), took exception to some fool thing I had written and forgot about.

"The Times took it serious and so did people arguing over it. They thought the fellow was some authority. Now what do I find out? He is a young Harvard graduate. And like all Harvard graduates, 'Junior' wanted to do something 'worth while' for the old alma mater.

"But America's sense of humor has taught 'em they is three things they must never take serious – columnist on any paper, a political speech by any candidate, and a Harvard graduate if he hasn't been out four years. Harvard is an eight-year school – four in and four out. But after then they are just human and fine as any college graduate.

"So, don't take the debt thing too serious from either Harvard or O.C.C. (Oklahoma Cow Camp). Their information on the subject is about equal." (Dec. 14, 1932.)

Even in times of economic struggles, a few more positive things do happen.

"Yesterday before breakfast the United States Treasury offered $850,000,000 worth of bonds and before the ham and eggs were reached they were all sold.

"That means sold and paid for, and salted away, not part paid for and the rest on margin till you sold 'em over the ticker to somebody else.

"If industry could interest some permanent buyers, like Roosevelt can in his business, then they could truly call themselves industrialists.

"As it is now, they are just manufacturing dice for Wall Street to shoot craps with. Nobody is buying a pair to keep." (Aug. 1, 1933.)

"Speaking at a banquet here (Chicago) tonight at the opening of a beautiful seventeen-story building built by the butter and egg men. It's a monument to the American people who can't tell a good egg from a bad one. It's a tribute to what a rooster and a churn can do.

"You can buy eggs on this market the same as you can buy General Motors stock. So, get you some eggs and hold 'em. Somebody will eat 'em no matter how old they are and if you can't pay your cold storage bill hardboil 'em and sell 'em for picnics." (April 25, 1928.)

Sometimes when things are bad, things are made worse because strikes are called, crippling the economy even more. In 2012, Greece is a good example. The national economy is staggering, so some unions there go on strike. Fortunately, in 2012, the United States was not facing any major strikes.

Unions try to do what they can to help their members – that's what they should do. But sometimes it might be better to look at the bigger interest, not just the local.

"Every week or so another fine plan comes from the administration.

"This last one of 'no strikes during these times and it's to be settled fairly by the government,' is one of the best yet.

"Unions are fine things, for they are in every line of business. Bankers have their association for mutual benefit. Governors have theirs. All big industries are bottled together in some way. But a strike should be the very last means for it is like war. It always falls on those who had nothing to do with it." (Aug. 6, 1933.)

"Both sides in the steel business seem anxious to strike.

Well, if they would only strike just each other it wouldn't be so bad.

"Don't it look like there ought to be some civilized way of finding out what the employee and the employer owed to each other?

"The latest papers say that 'It's up to the president now.' Is there any difficulty under the sun that's not put up to that man?" (June 7, 1934.)

Any time Will Rogers started talking about money and economics, he sooner or later hammered away at saving and avoiding credit.

"Don't make the first payment on anything. First payments is what made us think we were prosperous and the other nineteen is what showed us we were broke." ("Will Says.")

"We'll hold the distinction of being the only nation in the history of the world that ever went to the poor house in an automobile." ("Will Says.")

Sometimes you can find good advice where you least expect it.

"In order to see what little information I can pick up during these 'loco' days, I talk and ask questions of everyone I meet.

"Yesterday I run onto a fellow who had hitch-hiked his way out here from New York. Rather dignified looking old bird but kinder down at the heels. He give me about the most information I have had.

"He hopes they won't inflate. In fact, he hopes they will announce they will soon go back on gold, then everybody will know what their money is worth. Had optimistic helps of our future. Thought too many people, both large and small, looked too much to the government to fix their troubles, and do nothing themselves. He wasn't sore at the world, and had a good word for everybody.

"As I let him out of my car to catch a ride with someone else, I asked his name. Said his name was Baruch, Bernard Baruch.

"So pick up all old men you meet, some of 'em mightly smart." (Oct. 17, 1933.)

And then along comes some really good news:

"Here is the biggest news I have ever gathered. It's a real beat on the rest of the press.

"I have spent the whole day with Henry Ford, saw and drove in the new car. And here is what you have been waiting for for years, get ready, everybody.

"HE HAS CHANGED THE RADIATOR!

"I didn't even notice whether it has four wheels or five, two doors or twenty, whether it uses horses or is pulled by a motor. When I saw that radiator changed, I was just to tickled and overcome I couldn't tell you if the thing has got fenders or wings.

"I am to meet with him early in the morning again, and may be more composed. Then I can tell you tomorrow more about it. But what more would anybody want to know?" (Nov. 14, 1927.)

Back in Will Rogers's day, there was a lot of talk about the gold standard. What would they say if they saw the price of gold today?

"All I know is just what I read in the Albuquerque (N.M.) papers. They say we are off the gold.

"The best way to tell when each one of us went off the gold is to figure back how many years it was since we had any. Well, that's when we went off.

"The last I remember getting my clutches on gold was in

Johannesburg, South Africa; some five-dollar English gold pieces that we carried in a belt around our waist. I used the last one to pay a third-class passage to Australia, so I went off the gold in 1902.

"So this move strikes me as no great novelty or calamity." (April 20, 1933.)

Even so, he couldn't resist writing about gold.

"Going to buy gold on the world market now. What we been buying has been just 'home talent' gold.

"They claim the more you buy and the more you pay, the cheaper your dollar will get. Well, you will have no trouble on foreign support in this scheme. It will be no hardship for them to charge you even fifty dollars an ounce.

"So here is what us dumb ones don't get: When we had practically half the world's gold our dollar was still higher than a flagpole sitter.

"But this is no place for the ignorant, for there are two people you can't argue with. One is a professor, for he has specs, and the other is an economist, for he has a title." (Oct. 30, 1933.)

For some reason, Will Rogers sometimes did not seem to be a great fan of the Chamber of Commerce. The Chamber has long been a vital part of most local communities, but somewhere along the way Will got ruffled.

"The Chamber of Commerce of the United States that is in session in Washington now is running true to chamber of commerce form. They have the maximum of objections and all the minimum of remedies for all national ills. Of all the things that this country is suffering from, the greatest is overproduction of organizations organized to help somebody that don't need the help as bad as the organization itself. It's not taxes that keeps us flat. It's dues. When a failure, form something.

"When the judgment day comes half of America will be on their way up to some convention and the other half will be signing application blanks." (May 2, 1930.)

"Every paper every morning tells of a big gathering and prominent men who have spoken on 'Better Times.' If the Chambers of Commerce give some worker a job instead of some speaker at a dinner, there would be no unemployment.

"There has been more 'optimism' talked and less practiced than at any time during our history. Every millionaire we have has offered a speech instead of keeping still and offering a job. Our optimism is all at a banquet table, where everybody there has more than they can eat." (Oct. 24, 1930.)

He even brought the president at the time into it:

"There is one thing about this depression. It has offered every man, women and child in America 100 guesses on how to end it.

"President Hoover used up one of this guesses yesterday when he told one of those 'men's sewing clubs' (Chamber of Commerce, by the way, I think this was the mother lodge). He said we would 'have good times if everybody disarmed.'

"Why, that's the only people that are drawing salary now, is the army and navy. What does he want to do, put them among the unemployed?" (May 5, 1931.)

And then another president:

"There is no end to the blessings that this fellow Roosevelt has indirectly brought about.

"Orlando, Florida, has saw (or has seen) the light and has suspended six civic (eating) clubs and one Chamber of Commerce for sixty days.

"Now there is an injunction that should be made permanent. This country just civic luncheoned itself into depression. If they will all go home and eat with their own families, they will not only get their first good lunch in years, but will be surprised how much more intelligently their own wife can talk than the 'speaker of the day.'" (March 20, 1933.)

Chapter 8: Banks and People

Who's watching our money?

"Back here again today (Palo Alto, Cal.) looking for Mr. Hoover's house. Saw a sign 'to let' on it, so that don't look any too nourishing for you Democrats.

"Had a talk with Herbert this morning, not Herbert Hoover, but 'the' Herbert Fleischacker, who is the J.P. Morgan, Owen Young, Carter Glass and Andy Mellon, all combined, of the Pacific Coast.

"And, he is one rich man who didn't start out by saying, 'Well, I am an optimist.' He said, 'I don't know any more what's the matter with us, or what is going to happen to us, than the U.S. Senate does.'

"Imagine a big banker admitting to that?" (June 2, 1932.)

Bankers are in the money business, which one might suspect means that they make money available to others (at a price), right? Well, not always.

"Reluctant lenders and hesitant borrowers have contributed to a 7.4 percent drop in the amount of loans at area banks in the last year, according to lenders' most recent financial statements." – Mark Davis, in Kansas City Star, Dec. 13, 2011.

"No matter what the poor old dumb government tries to do, the 'big boys' have a scheme that beats it.

"Now the big bankers have got a new 'racket.' Instead of them going direct to the new finance commission for dough, they send the folks that owe them. He gets it from the government and then pays them off. That don't leave a single soul out snipe hunting with a sack but the government.

"And, brother, when one of those 'big babies' transfers one of his loans over to Uncle Sam, it's not a 'frozen asset,' it's a 'petrified persimmon.'" (March 29, 1932.)

Will Rogers soon found out that the bankers were not too happy with his criticisms of them:

"In one of my little poems I said the bankers were the first to go on the 'dole.' The 'wrath of the mighty' ascended on me. Even the Wall Street Journal (Wall Street's house organ) editorially said I should confine my jokes to some semblance of truth. Now I want to be fair, even with the bankers, for they are pretty touchy now. I have had critics come and say, 'As an actor old Bill is not so hot.' Well, I just wanted to come out and call him a liar, but in my heart and conscience I knew he was right. So I know how you 'boys' feel.

"Now, if you will take this money and loan it out to a lot of the little fellows that need it you bankers got a chance to redeem yourselves.

"But I am not kidding you. People are not 'pointing with pride' to your record in this crisis up to now. Will be glad to reprint any alibis." (March 10, 1932.)

Straying from bankers for a moment, Will turned his attention to something else.

"Well, they run all the racketeers out of Chicago, and they had not more than got them out till the Rotarians' convention got in. Now they are talking about letting the crooks come back. They figure they is some Rotarians here that could skin the crooks.

"You see, that organization only takes in the best in each line, so with all these new lines of commerce we have developed in the last few years, why they must have some pretty slick birds among 'em." (June 24, 1930.)

If nothing else, Will Rogers moved around a lot. Next stop, Boston:

"We been awful busy up here today celebrating Bunker Hill. Daniel Webster made the most famous Bunker Hill address, so I was really pinch hitting for him. He spoke good English, too. The Websters wrote all their own. You give me a chance to write my own dictionary and make a word mean anything I want it to, and I will show you some English.

"They are a broad-minded people up here. They celebrate a victory that the British won, and the monument is not on Bunker Hill – it's on Breed's Hill.

"But one thing they have got, and that's the old fighting ship Constitution – the only ship that has withstood every disarmament conference." (June 17, 1930.)

This is one time that Will was tripped up. He was writing about the wrong Webster, and it didn't take long before he heard about it.

"I said yesterday Daniel Webster wrote the dictionary. Well, these Harvardites have been calling me up before daylight telling me it was Noah Webster and not Daniel. How was I to know? I never read the book. I never could get interested in the thing.

"Well, anyhow the mistake will only be noticed in Boston." (June 18, 1930.)

From dictionaries to bankers again:

"The Bankers Institute (who call themselves the educational end of banking) are holding a big convention out here (Beverly Hills, Cal.). Every one of 'em carry American Express money orders. There is not a checkbook in a carload.

"I hope they go back by Canada and see how it is that Canada has only had one bank failure in ten years. The idea evidently is not copyrighted.

"But we can't alibi all our ills by just knocking the old banker. First he loaned the money, then the people all at once wanted it back, and he didn't have it. Now he's got it again, and is afraid to loan it, so the poor devil don't know what to do." (June 8, 1932.)

"I guess there is no two races of people in worse repute with everybody than the international bankers and the folks that put all those pins in new shirts." ("Will Says.")

"Banking and after dinner speaking are two of the most non-essential industries we have in this country. I am ready to reform if they are." ("Will Says.")

President Obama in 2011 and 2012 isn't the only president who had some difficulty with bankers:

"Big headlines in today's papers say that the big bankers, to show Roosevelt his financial scheme don't suit them, they are unloading government bonds and securities by the bushel. He won't play their way so they are going to sell their ball and bat and get out.

"I can't just recall, but as well as I remember, wasn't they the fellows that the government was helping so much not long ago? They ought to pray every night, 'God bless mama and papa, and all my family, and interests, and Roosevelt.'

"P.S. – I want to apologize to the president for putting interest ahead of him, but interest has been helping 'em out longer than he has." (Nov. 24, 1933.)

Too much red tape is always present in government and business. Will Rogers found a new problem.

"I see where a lot of banks are refusing the soldier boys loans on their adjusted compensations on account of too much red tape to handle. Not quite as much tape for them as it was to him to go to war, though there is at least no bullets in it.

"Thank goodness there will be no more wars. Now you tell one." (Jan. 6, 1927.)

According to accounts from Will Rogers, at least, bankers seem to have a lot of meetings.

"The American Bankers' Association are holding their annual benefit at Houston. It's their biggest benefit ever. The government has contributed permission for them to consolidate to freeze out the little fellow. The public, of course, will contribute everything else, so really the only problem before the convention is 'how much bonuses on loans will we make 'em pay above the legal rate of interest?'

"Branch banks are all the go now. They realize they have to bring the bank nearer the robber. He won't be annoyed by driving traffic just to rob one bank. The branch bank is the robbers' only salvation.

"P.S. – Every banker that could afford a failure in the last year is there." (Oct. 25, 1927.)

They are still at it:

"Guess who is out here (Beverly Hills) holding a convention, that would never thought would show their faces again? Yep, 'The Bankers.' The Reconstruction Finance Corporation fixed 'em up so they could make the trip.

"They are likeable rascals, and now that we are all wise to 'em, and it's been shown that they don't know any more about finances than the rest of us know about our business (which has proved to be nothing), why, they are getting just as human as the groceryman, the druggist or the filling station man.

"This panic has been a great equalizer, it's done away entirely with the smart man.

"So, the bankers are here having a good time. They don't feel that they have any position to uphold. They are just a lot of Elks." (Oct. 4, 1932.)

One more once:

"You can't get a room in Washington. Every hotel is jammed to the doors with bankers from all over America to get their 'handout' from the Dawes commission.

"And I have asked the following prominent men in America this question: 'What group have been more responsible for this financial mess – the farmer, labor, manufacturers, tradesmen, or who?'

"And every man, Henry Ford, Garner, Newt Baker, Borah, Curtis and a real financier, Bernard Baruch, and everyone of 'em without a moment's hesitation said: 'Why, the big bankers.'

"Yet they have the honor of being the first group to go on the 'dole' in America." (Feb. 24, 1932.)

Well, bankers actually do something besides go to conventions.

"I see where Jesse Jones and his R.F.C. (Redistribution Finance Corporation) are not satisfied with the way the banks are just sitting counting their money. So to make the banks ashamed of themselves the R.F.C. is going to make loans to industries. The banks will about be so humiliated that they will be the first ones to borrow all that Jesse has. Jesse, you been a banker yourself, you ought to know you can't shame a banker, especially a big one." (Dec. 18, 1933.)

Bankers certainly drew a lot of interest in those days, just as they do now, but Will Rogers had other things on his mind, too.

"When Jimmy Gerard said that fifty-seven men run this

country everybody thought it was an ad for Heinz pickles, so he had to add Bishop Cannon and Al Capone.

"Poor Jimmy – everybody jumped on his selections – everybody that wasn't mentioned. The Senate was broken-hearted in fact. The funny thing about the whole thing is, the ones that are running it don't want their names mentioned – not this year anyway. They are liable to sue Gerard for slander." (Aug. 28, 1930.)

Will was a man of many talents.

"As I paid for this joke, I want to see it in the papers. Right at Baltimore Friday in the big race I bet on four horses, all to win, place and show. Blue Coat was tipped me by Governor Ritchie, who I think was working on commission. One was called the 'Nut.'

"Well, birds of a feather must back each other. I bet on Earl Sande's Hermitage because Sande's my friend. Then there was a horse called Soul of Honor from Oklahoma; there's real humor for you.

"I had all these tickets in my outside coat pocket and some Republican senator or congressman pinched 'em. I discovered it just as they got to post, so my only hope was to pray for all of 'em to lose, and they did. They all four run last, so imagine that Republican scoundrel's embarrassment. The Lord was with us Democrats, but not often." (May 12, 1929.)

In addition to elected officials, Will often had thoughts about lawyers.

"Only one way you can beat a lawyer in a death case. That is to die with nothing." ("Will Says.")

"If it wasn't for wills, lawyers would have to go to work at an essential employment." ("Will Says.")

"Personally, I don't think you can make a lawyer honest by

an act of the legislature. You've got to work on his conscience. And his lack of a conscience is what makes him a lawyer." ("Will Says.")

Sometimes it is difficult to explain just where Will Rogers managed to come up with something.

"Now Mr. Hoover being a business man, I bet you he takes that Senate and House of Representatives space in the Capitol building and turns in into miniature golf courses.

"Would you believe it, there is 3,500 of 'em in the city of Los Angeles. Then people ask what's the matter with this country. Nothing, only there is millions got a 'putter' in their hand when they ought to have a shovel."

In this same daily Telegram, Will added another interesting observation:

"Half of America is bent over. In two more generations our children will grow upwards as far as their hips, then they will turn off at right angles and, with their arms hanging down, we will be right back when we started from.

"Darwin was right." (Aug. 5, 1930.)

No one could accuse Will Rogers of being dull.

"I guess our country holds the record for dumbness. The Pope spoke to the world this morning in three languages and we didn't understand a one of 'em. But the minute he finished and the local stations got back to selling corn salve and pyorrhea tooth paste we were right up our intellectual alley again.

"A real prince of Japan will visit Los Angeles tomorrow, but he picked a bad time to come, for on the same day Aimee gets in here from one of her pilgrimages, and any time Aimee returns home from somewhere, even if it's just from the desert, why this town goes practically ga-ga." (May 15, 1931.)

"The Lord so constituted everybody that no matter what

color you are, you require the same amount of nourishment."
("Will Says.")

"I am no believer in this 'hard work, perserverance, and taking advantage of your opportunities' that these magazines are so fond of writing some fellow up in. The successful don't work any harder than the failures. They get what is called in baseball the breaks." ("Will Says.")

"Indians and primitive races were the highest civilized because they were more satisfied and they depended less on each other and took less from each other." ("Will Says.")

Unlike so many others who made movies, Will did not talk about how wonderful he was.

"Breakfast this morning at Beverly Hills and dinner tonight at Wichita. Plane full of passengers and fine trip. In the morning will just hop down home to Claremore. They was opening my first talking picture tonight in Los Angeles and charging those poor people five dollars, and I just couldn't stand by and be a party to such brigandage. First-night audiences pay their money to look at each other, so if they get stuck tomorrow night, they can't blame me. It will be because they don't look good to each other." (Sept. 17, 1929.)

Will liked to make fun of lawyers, but he had a different attitude toward doctors.

"All doctors should make enough out of those who are well able to pay to be able to do all work for the poor free. One thing that a poor person should never be expected to pay for is medical attention and not from an organized charity but from our best doctors. Your doctor bill should be paid like your income tax, according to what you have." ("Will Says.")

"Best doctor in the world is the veterinarian. He can't ask

his patients what's the matter. He's just got to know." ("Will Says.")

Will did not go too far in formal schooling and it would seem that he had some doubts about higher education.

"The papers today say that illiteracy has decreased. The more that learn how to read the less learn how to make a living. That's one thing about a little education, it spoils you for actual work. The more you know the more you think somebody owes you a living." (Sept. 4, 1931.)

"Villains are getting as thick as college degrees and sometimes on the same fellow." ("Will Says.")

"The wets have just shown that you can get a drink, and it's bad for the country. Now the drys start, and will show that you can't get a drink, and it's good for the country.

"In the meantime, there is at least 90,000,000 living in the country that it's not affecting in any way and that wish that both sides would shut up and go to work.

"If papers announced that they would quit printing what either side said, the 90,000,000 would feel so relieved that they would celebrate with a grand spree and then sober up for the rest of their lives." (March 5, 1930.)

Maybe Will was a little tough on college people, but he did have some good words for a rural teacher.

"America is a land of opportunity and don't ever forget it.

"Yesterday out here in Los Angeles (where our local papers say people are dying from heat by the thousands in the East) out here we are just dying but for no particular reason at all, well there was elected to a very high office, president of the Educational Association, just a plain pleasant looking fat (and enjoying it) common sense woman. She is head of the rural schools in Maine and when you are rural in Maine you are rural. Now she is head of all the teachers in our land.

"I guess from her name, 'Miss," that she is an old maid, but, darn it, I just liked her looks in the paper this morning and I believe she could teach these young modern heathens of ours some sense." (July 1, 1931.)

Chapter 9: Politics

It ain't what you know. . .

"Well, the old gentlemanly game of politics is just starting to hit her stride.

"Roosevelt in his Ohio speech gave seven points where he would remedy things. The Hoover bunch are trying to get the market up seven points so this is a seven-point campaign.

"The minute one side makes a speech, the humorously called 'strategists' on the other side go into a huddle to pick it apart, which all don't mean a thing.

"Politicians amuse more people than they interest." (Aug. 22, 1932.)

There has been an ongoing discussion – if not debate – for years over whether or not the primary elections for presidential nominees are worth the money and trouble. Nothing has been decided, but Will pointed out one option:

"Oklahoma and Texas have an original primary system.

"They have so many seeking office that the first primary is only to find out how many are desirous of living off the state.

"The second primary is to eliminate 50 per cent of these.

"The third is to get rid of half of what is left.

"The fourth is to eliminate any good man that might have crept in by mistake.

"Now, you have just politicians, so the fifth one is to leave in the two worst ones, and they run it off." (July 30, 1930.)

On several occasions Will offered his explanations of what politics what was all about:

"You could keep politics clean if you could figure out some way so your government never hired anyone." ("Will Says.")

"All there is to politics is trading. That's why politics is not as good as it was years ago. They don't have as many old-time horse traders in there. These we got are just amateurs. They're crude with their trades. There is really no 'finesse.' You might not get that. 'Finesse' is a French word and it means sneaking it over." ('Will Says.")

"Politics is the only sporting event in the world where they don't pay off for second money; a man to run second in any other event in the world it's an honor. But any time he runs second for president it's not an honor. It's a pity." ("Will Says.")

Will even went so far as to blame prohibition for the sad condition of politics.

"Prohibition originally started out with us a moral issue. It was either good or bad for you to drink. Then it drifted to economics: Did people save more when not drinking? Then into racketeering. But now it's drifted into the worst angle of any, that is politics. American history records no return of anything once it got into politics.

"The vote in the Senate the other day shows that morals, economy, less taxes, nothing entered their minds; only 'how can my party get part of the beer and all the credit?' Beer has lined up with the post offices as political loot." (July 15, 1932.)

Even though he was a Democrat himself, Will often took jabs at both the Republicans and the Democrats.

"The Democrats are having a lot of fun exposing the Republican campaign corruptions, but they would have a lot more fun if they knew where they could lay their hands on some of it themselves for next November." ("Will Says.")

"A flock of Democrats will replace a mess of Republicans. It won't mean a thing. They will go in like all the rest of 'em. Go in on promises and come out on alibis." ("Will Says.")

"The platform will always be the same, promise everything, deliver nothing." ("Will Says.")

Will even took jabs at the conventions and cities where they held them, but he always seemed to show up for the activities.

"Can you imagine? This town of Cleveland wants the Republican and Democratic conventions both in 1928.

"A town that don't know any more than that is liable to ask for a sesquicentennial. The Republican convention will be held further West, for that's the way they are going to relieve the farmers – to let 'em see a convention. And as for the Democratic one, a sanity test will follow any town purposely asking for it." (April 15, 1927.)

It takes money to make money.

"No wonder the Republican party in this country is careful to do nothing to interfere with big banking interests. Look over in England. The Labor party was in but they had no money. They get out and a different bunch in New York and Paris banks loaned 'em a half billion dollars.

"Big money only goes to the party that supports big money. I am entering no crusade to end it. I am just telling you how it is. You go ahead and change it." (Aug. 28, 1931.)

"The more I see of politics. . . the more I wonder what in the world any man would ever want to take it up for. Then some people wonder why the best men of a community are not the office holders." ("Will Says.")

"I generally give the party in power, whether Republican or Democrat, the more digs because they are generally doing the country more damage. The party in power drawing a salary is to be knocked." ("Will Says.")

The Republican party is holding so many debates among presidential candidates in 2012 that the voters can't tell who's on first. It's not so much a campaign of issues, it's more of a race to see which candidate can stick his foot in his mouth the most. One has to wonder: just how important are these primaries anyhow?

"Maine holds the first election every year (this was in 1930). They hold it for the reason there is an old saying, as goes Maine, so goes the country.

"Well, they held it a couple of days ago and nobody has been interested enough in it to ask how it went. Nobody voted, only the candidates that was running.

"People ain't anymore interested in politics than they are in long underwear. Both sides have lied to 'em so often that we don't look on either candidate with admiration or with hate. We just pity 'em." (Sept. 9, 1930.)

After all these debates and primary elections, the Republicans and Democrats will move on to their presidential conventions.

"Today being Sunday (even in a political convention), I just got an idea I would see just how religious all these politicians really are, as I had heard that religion might play some part in the Fall festivities. So I grab a cab and rush from one church to the other all over town, and not a single delegate, or even delegates, was among the worshipers.

"Still, this Fall, in the campaign, you will hear them get up and shout 'Our religion is the bulwark of our great and glorious country; we must continute to be God-fearing people; our Church is our salvation.' Well, our churches are our salvation, but some of those babies won't be among the rescued." (June 10, 1928.)

The year was 1928 and that particular convention was being held in Kansas City. It wasn't all politics, however.

"Bank was robbed just before the convention opened

this morning. Chicago and Indiana delegations are under surveillance.

"Young Bob La Follette made the only real speech that has been made at the convention. He spoke in favor of the people. He was listened to, but his amendments were not adopted. They kept in the Wall Street ones. If there is enough banks to rob, there is no telling when the convention will adjourn." (June 14, 1928.)

Maybe they don't accomplish too much, but politicians sure know how to make speeches.

"It's too bad there's not some machine or way of registration just how many votes a political speech gets or loses. I claim if we had some way of finding out it would do away with political speeches.

"Coolidge made less speeches and got more votes than any man that ever ran. Bryan was listened to and cheered by more people than any single human in politics, and he lost. So there is a doubt whether just talking does you good or harm." (Sept. 21, 1928.)

"When an office holder, or one that has been found out, can't think of anything to deliver a speech on, he always falls back on the good old subject, AMERICANISM." ("Will Says.")

Will Rogers tries to distinguish between Republicans and Democrats.

"It takes nerve to be a Democrat, but it takes money to be a Republican."

"Democrats take the whole thing as a joke. Republicans take it serious but run it like a joke."

"The Republican platform promises to do better. I don't think they have done so bad. Everybody's broke but them."

Unemployment was a big thing in 1932, just as it is in 2012:

"We never realized that elections were so near till we saw by the papers this morning that each political party has 'some' plan of relieving the unemployed.

"They have been unemployed for three years, and nobody paid any attention to 'em, but now both parties have discovered that while they are not working there is nothing in the Constitution to prevent them from voting.

"So Democratic Campaign Leader 'Hooey' and Republican Leader 'Baloney' say:

"'We have to do something about this, Miss Secretary, reach in the bag and get out some of those old campaign promises. We will dust 'em off and use 'em again this year, and remember no matter what the other side promises, see their promise and raise 'em two more." (June 6, 1932.)

More observations by Will about the political parties:

"If a man wants to stand well socially, he can't afford to be seen with either the Democrats or the Republicans."

"There ain't any finer folks living than a Republican that votes the Democratic ticket."

"Republicans want a man that can lend dignity to the office. Democrats want a man that will lend some money."

Will didn't think much of political claims about being prosperous.

"Of all the 'dumb' issues that candidates bring up to try and influence people how to vote, I think 'prosperity' takes the cake. How a speaker can convince a man that he is prosperous when he is broke or that he is not prosperous when he is doing well is beyond me. If a voter can't feel in his pocket and see if he is doing well without having some total stranger tell him, then his government shouldn't be in the hands of the people. We might as well have candidates argue with us that we have a pain in our stomach." (Oct. 29, 1928.)

Will ponders a letter to some governors.

"The governors of all the states are gathered together in Connecticut to show how far apart they are. Mr. Wickersham sent a letter to them and, like everything that a highly educated man writes, nobody could understand what he meant. They don't know from it if he is wet, dry, damp, repeal, enforce, endure, modify or let bad enough alone. They have tried to ask him 'what he meant,' and he can't tell 'em. The letter has had one outstanding outcome. It's made Secretary Caraway a Democrat and Senator Borah a dissolutionist. Both see a thing the same way. They agree that Wickersham is all wet." (July 19, 1929.)

"We cuss the lawmakers. But I notice we're always perfectly willing to share in any of the sums of money that they might distribute."

"No element, no party, not even Congress or the Senate can hurt this country now; it's too big. That's why I can never take a politician seriously."

"There is no more independence in politics than there is in jail. They are always yapping about 'public service.' It's public jobs that they are looking for."

Will pays tribute to George Washington on George's birthday.

"Here is what George Washington missed by not living to his 199th birthday.

"He would have seen out great political system of 'equal rights to all and privileges to none' working so smoothly that 7,000,000 are without a chance to earn their living.

"He would see 'em handing out rations in peacetime that would have reminded him of Valley Forge. In fact, we have reversed the old system. We all get fat in war times and thin during peace.

"I bet after seeing us he would sue us all for calling him 'Father.'" (Feb. 22, 1931.)

While Will liked to poke fun at politicians, sometimes he admitted they weren't all so bad:

"None of them from any party are going to purposely ruin the country. They will all do the best they can."

But then he realized he was talking about politics:

"You've go to admit that each party is worse than the other. The one that's out always looks the best."

"A politician is just like a pickpocket. It's almost impossible to get one to reform."

"No mathematician in this country has ever been able to figure out how many hundred straw votes it takes to equal one legitimate vote."

"No animal in the world gets quite as hungry as a Democrat. He would rather make a speech than a dollar."

If you can't beat 'em, join 'em:

"Say, I got a great new political scheme. Captain Hickman, captain of the Texas Rangers, wants me to run as vice president on the Democratic ticket, me being Cherokee Indian, and Charley Curtis a Kaw Indian.

"Hickman's theory is that the Cherokees have licked the Kaws, and that there is many more Cherokees than Kaws. Pretty sound reasoning, and besides, nobody knows how I stand on prohibition. Coolidge was president six years and nobody knew how he stood. Religion – I am a holy roller. Farm relief, I never voted for, against or even read the Mary McHaughen bill.

"Vote for Rogers and scalp the Kaws." (June 22, 1928.)

Don't believe all these political experts, Will warns.

"Of all the comical things, the so-called local party leaders take the cake. Smith's leaders have assured him he will carry every state he has gone into. Meaning he could carry all of them, but he don't like to travel so much. Moses, the Republican apostle, told Hoover today that Smith wouldn't get ten votes even on Oliver Street, and that Hoover was a cinch for everything east of the Golden Gate, and a chance for a split in Honolulu.

"How do they know what people are going to do? You would think they had a sworn affidavit of every voter. Of all the 'yes' men they are the prize. If either candidate believes one half of 1 per cent what any of his henchmen say, then Hoover or Smith neither one are smart enough to be president." (Oct. 27, 1928.)

Ah, for the good old days.

"Washington's birthday – Hear the political speeches delivered under the guise of being addresses on Washington! They will start out by saying that, 'It's the birthday of our first president. Had he lived to see the fruits of the great Republican party –'

"As a matter of fact, there wasn't any Republicans in Washington's day. No Republicans, no boweevil, no income tax, no cover charge, no disarmament conference, no luncheon clubs, no stop lights, no static, no head winds. Liquor was a companion, and not a problem. No margins, no ticket speculators, no golf pants or Scotch jokes, and Tom hadn't yet read about the iniquities of Rome.

"Lord, living in those times, who wouldn't be great?" (Feb. 21, 1929.)

From time to time Will returned to Oklahoma. One time he was in Ponca City:

"Well, Oklahoma had a great day here today. Mr. Hoover opened our ceremonies from Washington, in payment for the state going Republican the last election, then Pat Hurley, our unanimously most popular Oklahoman and Secretary of War, from a sick bed in Washington, made a radio talk to us that would have done credit to a Democrat.

"It was a wonderful gathering, all our present and impeached governors were there, there was a tremendous crowd. Ah, folks, you can act, and talk, and do stunts, all over the world, but the applause of a home audience is sweeter to your ears than anything in the world." (April 22, 1930.)

A few more comments from Will about politics:

"I love animals and I love politicians. I like to watch both of 'em play either back home in their native state or after they have been captured and sent to a zoo or to Washington."

"I have looked politics and the movies both over and, while they have much in common and I believe politics is the most common, so I will stay with the movies."

"The truth can hurt you worse in an election than about anything that could happen to you."

Ever so often someone would urge Will Rogers to run for political office. This usually made him scramble and scratch around, trying to smother the talk. After several efforts to stop such talk, in 1931 Will made a serious effort:

"Will you do me one favor? If you see or hear of anybody proposing my name either humorously or semiseriously for any political office, will you maim said party and send me the bill?

"Life magazine and I had a lot of fun last time by running for office, but am certainly not going to try and impose the same comedy twice.

"My friend on Collier's (George Creel it is, by the way, that writes that clever 'Keyhole Column' in Collier's) says that I am taking this running serious. George, that's the worst slam you ever took against my sense of humor.

"I certainly know that a comedian can only last till he either takes himself serious or his audience takes him serious, and I don't want either one of those to happen to me till I am dead (if then).

"So let's stop all this damned foolishness right now. I hereby and hereon want to go on record as being the first presidential, vice-presidential, senator or justice of peace candidate to withdraw. I not only 'don't choose to run' but I don't ever want to want to leave a loophole in case I am drafted, so I won't use 'choose.' I will say 'won't run' no matter how bad the country will need a comedian by that time. I couldn't run anyhow, because I can't make up my mind which side to run on, 'wet' or 'dry.' I don't know which side the most votes is on and I can't straddle it, for that's where all the rest of the candidates are now.

"I hope in doing this that I have started something that will have far reaching effect. Who will be the next to do the public a favor and withdraw? What is there to worry anybody over the next nomination anyhow? It's one year away, but the candidates will be Hoover and Curtis versus Franklin D. Roosevelt and some Western or Southern Democratic governor as vice president." (June 28, 1931.)

Will offers a few comments about politics and politicians:

"A statesman is a man that can do what the politician would like to do but can't because he is afraid of not being elected."

"Once a man wants to hold a public office, he is absolutely no good for honest work."

"This country has gotten where it is in spite of politics, not by the aid of it."

Women are getting more active in politics, according to Will:

"The whole campaign has switched from Hoover and Smith to Mrs. Willebrandt. Now, I used to think that no one in the world could possibly make a poorer speech than some man politician, but after attending both conventions and various dinners and public affairs, I have found that any woman politician can make a poorer political speech than man any time they try. I don't know why it is but it just looks like the wrong women are in politics, for I have heard other women on other subjects make brilliant speeches. I believe their cause would get further if they would just vote and not try to explain publicly why." (Sept. 27, 1928.)

For once, Will found a speech he liked:

"Hoover dug up a whole new subject last night, and made the best speech of his campaign.

"It was about keeping Congress and the Senate from having anything to do with the nation's business. If he had gone a step further and come out for the entire abolishment, I believe he would have been elected unanimously on the spot.

"Smith is always saying, 'If I get in I will appoint a commission to look into so and so.' That's what fills poorhouses – people that have waited for some government committee to act.

"Outside of traffic, there is nothing that has held this country back as much as committees." (Oct. 23, 1928.)

A few more comments about politics:

"A cannibal is a good deal like a Democrat, they are forced to live off each other."

"What this country needs is more working men and fewer politicians."

"Politics ain't worrying this country one tenth as much as parking space."

Will decided to get away from politics for a while.

"No papers away out here (Vernon, Texas) on the prairie where I am, so I don't know what has happened.

"By golly, to people away out on farms and ranches, where

people make a living off what you are supposed to make it off of, why it don't make much difference what happens. The 'market could have closed strong,' or closed forever, and it wouldn't matter to a big bunch of Americans.

"It sure is a lot prettier sight to look at thousands of white-faced cattle than thousands of bald-faced delegates in one corral howling like mad and milling for nothing.

"They brand the cattle so you can tell 'em, and have to put bandages on the delegates, so there's not much difference after all." (July 7, 1932.)

Chapter 10: Sports

All work and no play. . .

"The Alabama Bo-Weevils destroyed Washington Apple Knockers at Pasadena yesterday. Washington had all red suits, shoes, pants, helmets and all. They looked like eleven bottles of strawberry pop.

"The score sounded like the Democratic convention at Madison Square Garden. 'Alabama votes 24 for Underwood.'

"Here is the best one that happened in the Rose Festival yesterday: A policeman arrested some little boys for plucking roses from a yard at the house Einstein, the great scientist, is stopping at. The kids then showed the policeman that the roses were not growing; they were tied on all sorts of bushes with strings. That's one of California's theories that Einstein don't understand." (Jan. 2, 1931.)

Will Rogers was an ardent participator in polo, and taught his children to play the game. This, of course, went right along with his passion for riding horses and roping. He also followed major sports, and became friends with many of the top names in sports. It would be interesting to see his reaction to one of the new names capturing sports headlines in 2011 and 2012.

"Go ahead and 'Tebow.' You know: crouch on one knee, put your fist to your forehead and close your eyes in prayer as Denver Broncos quarterback Tim Tebow does during NFL games." – Sean Gregory, in Dec. 19, 2011, *Time.*

Will Rogers demonstrated a love for football, and also some insight into the sport.

"Dr. Mayo and his accomplices held spring practice on the body of Knute Rockne, the Notre Dame coach. They extracted some of his poison and give it to rabbits and waited to see their death. Instead, the rabbits went into a huddle, came out with an Easter egg. A little 'Irish' cottontail named Gonsolovitch started heaving forward passes with this egg with a Belgian hare called (for gate receipt purposes) Murphy. Eight Australian jack-rabbits run interference for him. Mayo then took a larger dose of this poison from Knute's infected leg and gave it to eleven little baby guinea pigs. They immediately defeated the rabbits, 58 to 0.

"Then both teams wound up by going to mass to Father Duffy." (April 25, 1930.)

Will noticed that other nations also play football.

"After a football game in Lima, Peru, five were killed. They only kill ten in a revolution down there, so two games equals one revolution.

"Up here we don't kill our football players. We make coaches out of the smartest ones and send the others to the Legislature." (Jan. 5, 1931.)

Sometimes Will wrote about other sports.

"Helen Wills, we saw your picture in that court dress. Get back into those tennis rompers quick. It looked like the Statue of Liberty with an ostrich fan instead of a lantern. Let the queen come to you.

"I got the wrong outfit broadcasting the Kentucky Derby. The announcer was seeing his first race, he knew horses like I know Homer and Shakespeare: 'Collitetti wins, ridden by Jockey Naishpur; Exterminator second. No, they are putting the floral wreath on Larkspur, a niece of Man o' War. We will now take you back to the studio where Texas Guinan will recite "Black Bess."'" (May 19, 1929.)

Sometimes Will wondered just how important football rated on some university campuses.

"The football season is on and here is as pathetic a note as I ever read. It's by Gil Dobie, head coach at Cornell.

"The future of Cornell as a Class A college is entirely in the hands of the faculty. If they are going to be bullheaded and insist on the students studying and carrying on a lot of lessons and getting their minds and time off what they are here for, why we will finish where all other narrow-minded colleges finish, in the cellar.

"But if they wake up like Notre Dame, California and Princeton, and realize it's touchdowns we want, and not degrees, it's future coaches we want to turn out, and not college presidents, then only will Cornell return to its proud place among prosperous universities.

"But I can do nothing. It's all in the hands of the faculty." (Sept. 19, 1929.)

And another musing:

"Harvard and Yale played Saturday, as usual to decide which was the worst team in America. Harvard students have completed more English courses and less forward passes than any school in this generation. They got correspondence school teams out West here that they have to handcuff to keep them from going and beating Harvard and Yale." (Nov. 21, 1926.)

And another:

"Dr. Wilce, the Ohio State coach, just showed me their new stadium, seating 100,000, built by hard study and excellent scholarship.

"They can seat 200 students to every book in the university. They lost to Michigan by a kick after touchdown. He has 400 students practicing day and night in relays to kick goals.

"A product of the old book mode of education.

"P.S. – I suggested they practice making another touchdown, then they wouldn't have to worry about the goal kicking." (Jan. 14, 1927.)

And one more:

"The football season is about over. Education never had a more financial year. School will commence now.

"Successful colleges will start laying plans for new stadiums; unsuccessful ones will start hunting a new coach; cheer leaders will join the Rotary luncheons for hog-calling contests. Heroes have been cheered that will never do anything to be cheered again.

"We are trying to arrange a post-season game between Harvard and the motion-picture leading men." (Nov. 30, 1927.)

And then there was this story about a runner:

"It's about time somebody give a real endurance test some credit – this foot race to New York, and a 20-year-old kid from Claremore, Okla., leading it. It's all right to kid it and call it bunions, but no athlete in any other branch of sport could get up every day for three straight months and run from forty to seventy miles.

"Sporting writers write pages over some football player's seventy-yard run. Our champion prize fighters can only fight thirty minutes every two years. There is not a golf player in America that could have stood this same trip in an automobile. You will find it's the grit and heart that's doing this more than bunions or ingrowing toe nails, so be fair and give 'em a break." (May 14, 1928.)

Some holidays reminded Will of football.

"Today was Armistice Day, celebrated to commemorate the end of a slaughter. There were more casualties in football games

113

celebrating the Armistice than there were before the Armistice was declared. We got enough people for another war but not enough to stand another Armistice Day. But football is not nearly so devastating as the Armistice Day oratory. If we fought like we declaimed we would be repaying reparations." (Nov. 11, 1926.)

Somebody ought to stand up for that poor college guy who was ridiculed so much for running the wrong way with a football. Who else but Will Rogers?

"Everybody is a-picking on that poor boy out there in California that run the wrong way with that football. If I was an editorial writer like Mr. Hearst, Mr. Brisbane, Bruce Barton, Glenn Frank and all of those, I would ask how many out of the hundred and ten million of the rest of us are headed the wrong way? How many out of us have even had presence of mind enough to pick up a fumble? How many grabbed out of the scramble what they think is success and don't know till they reach the goal line whether it's the right one or not.

"So come on, preachers, hop on this as your text. All I want is 10 per cent of that Sunday's collection to get this boy a medal for at least doing something different from one million other college boys. Even if it was wrong, his mind wasn't standardized." (Jan. 3, 1929.)

Speaking of collecting money:

"The Carnegie Foundation got their answer about paid athletes who were subsidized. One-half million people attended seven games where the athletes were subsidized. Less than half that many attended fifty games where the athletes were pure, but not much athletes. The public don't care how you got to a college, it's how are you going to get from the 40-yard line to over the goal that they are worrying over.

"We are a 'get the dough' people, and our children are born

in a commercial age. Why if a babe in arms can cry loud enough to get paid for it we are tickled to death. Make 'em pay for talent whether it's art, music, football, literature, radio announcing or flag pole sitting.

"Any actors that can draw 88,000 people in one day is worthy of their hire. Don't let Wall Street get all the gravy." (Oct. 27, 1929.)

Those irritating interruptions for commercials and program promos while you try to watch television drive everyone nuts – including Will Rogers (and they didn't even have TV in his day):

"I don't know what it's the height of, but it sho is the height of something terrible, and that is when forty million people have been listening intently to Graham McNamee for two hours describe a thrilling World Series game and then hear: 'We will now switch you back to the studio for the Safety Can Opener Hour, where you will be highly entertained by Sarah Wow, who will whine for you that ditty, "I Just Don't Believe I Can Prevent Myself from Caring in a Small Way for That Steaming, Broiling, Half-Burned Man of Mine," after which those Harmonizing Hounds will entertain you during Rosenbaum's Catchup Hour.'" (Oct. 13, 1929.)

Will really did like baseball.

"That was a mighty fine thing of President and Mrs. Hoover, going clear to Philadelphia to see that baseball game. Baseball is still and always will be our national game. It requires more brains, more practice and more real skill than all our others put together. It's the only game when you see it played you know whether the ones playing are being paid or not.

"There was twenty million baseball fans that listened to the World Series that knew every play made, and why, and how it was made, but still don't know whether Harvard is a town or a mouth wash, whether Yale is a yell or a lock, and think all Notre Dames are churches.

"So viva baseball. It's for us unfortunate ones who have no alumni." (Oct. 14, 1929.)

"Baseball is in for a great year. It's our national game and will always be our national game. We become a great nation under baseball and commenced to flop the minute we started to take up a lot of poor substitutes." ("Will Says.")

Will certainly loved horses, so maybe it's natural that he should notice horse racing.

"Well they had the big horse race out here (Santa Monica, Cal.) Saturday. For the most money any race ever paid, and an Irish horse won it. He was seven years old. He had been a steeplechase horse and he was Saturday. He jumped over 20 American horses.

"There was eight hundred thousand dollars bet at that track on the eight races. The stores of Los Angeles put on a dollar sale and they played to more money than the races did, and Iowa had a picnic the same day out here and they had more people than the races and the dollar sale combined.

"With all these going on in one town, I wouldn't worry too much about the country going Bolsheviki." (Feb. 24, 1935.)

Or how about a different kind of racing?

"Did you ever drive one of these 'sulkys' in a trotting race? Well, they got old David Harum sitting straddle of a horse's tail out here on the Riverside track, and if you think that hasn't got it on all auto driving you are wrong.

"I am getting just about old enough and crabbed enough to take up the Grand Circuit. So look out Goshen and Lexington, young Pop Geers is coming East.

"We have our radios, autos, golf, bridge and a million

contraptions, but all of it don't pay for the thrill missed in stepping out in the red wheel buggy and high stepper.

"You could be a pretty poor type of lover, but the horse made up for it. That's how a lot of us was able to go out of our class and get the wives we did." (Jan. 10, 1934.)

Will didn't just watch polo games, he was a good player himself. And he liked to gloat sometimes:

"Well, the 'hill billies' beat the 'dudes' and took the polo championship of the world right out of the drawing rooms and into the bunk house.

"She won't go East in years, for the West always thought you had to have a birth certificate to play it. Now every cowpuncher is herding in the heifers with a corn-plaster saddle and even the 'hay-heavers' have changed a pitchfork into a polo mallet.

"Twenty thousand Chicagoans witnessed Sunday's social massacre. Nineteen thousand of 'em had never seen a horse, much less a polo game.

"So from now on west of the Mississippi 'Old Dobbbin' plows in the field only till 4 o'clock, when he will be washed, scrubbed and his teeth polished and he goes out on the lawn to cavort in what used to be known as strictly a social recreation.

"Poor old society, they got nothing exclusive left. The movie folks outmarried and outdivorced 'em, the common folks took their cocktails, 'near' society took to bridge. Now polo has gone to the buckwheat belt, so poor old society hasn't even been left a code." (Aug. 21, 1933.)

Will Rogers also had an interest in golf.

"This country is not entirely over the 'cuckoo' stage yet, for every day there is more printed in the papers about the new and old golf ball than there is on unemployment. When the dimensions of a golf ball is our greatest worry, we still got a long way to go to get back to normal. Five thousand people followed Bobby Jones and watched him watch the golf championship. We ought to get Bobby to sit in Washington and watch it. That might revive interest in our present form of government." (Sept. 1, 1931.)

"Golf is the only game in the world where it takes longer to explain than it does to play."

There are lots of top golfers today, and millions watch them every week on television. In Will Rogers's day, the top golfer was an amateur named Bobby Jones.

"What can we do for this Bobby Jones that keeps monotonously winning all these golf championships? I would propose him for president, but I haven't got it in for him that bad. On the golf course it's just your opponents that are shooting at you, but it looks like in the White House your friends are the ones you got to watch." (June 20, 1930.)

"Atlanta no more than gets cleaned up from one Bobby Jones celebration till another comes along. You can easily exist in Atlanta by eating only at Jones's testimonial dinners. If all Jones's banquet speakers were laid end to end it would make a fairway with a 287 par. So find a spot on Stone Mountain for Bobby. Had he lived in the days of Jeff Davis, Stonewall Jackson and Robert E. Lee, he would have done to Grant and Sheridan what he did to Hagan, Diegel and Sarazen.

"And just think, ten years ago all Atlanta had was Coca Cola." (July 13, 1930.)

But there was more to golf than Bobby Jones.

"Just passed by one of our fine country clubs out here (California) and there was a big crowd there. It was the woman's golf championship of America. We used to think going to see women play golf would be like going to see men crochet, but, say, there is nothing effeminate about this golf thing as played by these champion women. Say, what a bunch of Channel swimmers they are! I would hate to beat one of them to a parking space. They just put that innocent little ball down, grit their teeth and swing like a woodchopper, and it takes one of our modern men in mighty good physical condition to even walk where it goes. Miniature golf might be all right for men, but not for this humorously called weaker sex." (Oct. 17, 1930.)

And of course there was always baseball.

"With the baseball season opened and Washington headed for another pennant, boy, Congress better be good from now on!

"Golf is played for conversational purposes. Polo is played by us lazy ones, because the horse does all the work and we love to just go for the ride.

"But you have to play baseball for itself alone, for there is no clubhouse to talk it over in after the game.

"From an old first baseman of the Oologah (Okla.) Giants." (April 17, 1934.)

Or one could always turn to football.

"Well, let's see what we got in today's papers that will hold up till tomorrow.

"Huey Long (Huey will stand up) is trying to make senators out of football players. He better be trying to make something out of senators. I don't blame that boy for not wanting to be demoted.

"Awful lot of predictions in the papers every day as to what is the outlook for political success in 1936. The ins, and the outs, too, better concentrate on what's going to happen next month or next week. No country in the world was ever further away from 1936 than we are." (Nov. 13, 1934.)

Chapter 11: Farmers and Farming

Here are the real people. . .

"Farm Board destroying every third row of cotton is the nub of a great idea. What would give more relief than extinguishing every third senator, every third congressman, every third committee, every third stock broker, every third law. Make a third of the vice presidents of concerns go back to work. Turn the cows back into every third golf course. Convict every third gangster arrested. One-third of all millionaires that issue optimistic reports from aboard yachts. Too many banks, bump off a third. Stop up every third oil well and every third political speaker.

"Destroy one-half the newspaper columnists, and last, but the main thing, the matter with the whole world is there is too many people. Shoot every third one. This whole plan is inexpensive and a sure-fire scheme back to prosperity." (Aug. 16, 1931.)

Maybe Will's plan is a trifle extreme, but he was very sympathetic toward the farmers. He considered himself one of them, although he was more of a rancher than farmer.

"Farmers are having a tough time but they had no idea they were so bad off till they joined an organization and had some paid leaders tell 'em how poor they are.

"If ever an industry was having a field day, it's the industry of paid leaders in every line, who are explaining to their followers 'what the government owes them.'

"I haven't seen a copy of the Constitution in years (I guess they are out of print), but I don't remember in there anything about what it was to do if you raised too much, or if you manufactured too much, or if you went into debt too much, or if you drove your automobile too much, or if you bathed in one of your bathrooms too much.

"If fact, if I remember right, we owed more to the Constitution than it did to us." (Oct. 23, 1933.)

Will was serious about this idea of too many leaders doing more harm than good.

"Up in Dingville, Iowa, named for the great cartoonist Ding and sometimes called Des Moines, the farmers and the governors are in convention.

"It don't take a convention to tell that the farmers are in a bad plight.

"The speeches were all made by farm leaders. Now what is a farm leader? I was raised on a farm. We had farm hands, farm hired girls, farm horses, farm mortgages, (not many) but I never saw a farm that raised farm leaders.

"This leader thing is a type of growth that has sprung up since everybody started joining organizations, not only in farming but in everything.

"In the old days if you was smart enough to be in a business, you was smart enough to tend to your own business without listening to a leader make a speech.

"Yours for less leaders and less followers of leaders." (Nov. 1, 1933.)

Farmers need help in many years. Back in Will Rogers's day, there was a thing called "relief."

"One thing about farmers' relief: It can't last long, for the farmers ain't got much more to be relieved of." ("Will Says.")

Naturally, the politicians rushed to the rescue.

"As I write it's pretty near farm relief time. About 8 o'clock every night they get relief over the radio. Last night Smith marketed their surpluses at a profit for 'em. Tonight, Hoover, through cooperative marketing, will assist them in payments on new cars. Then tomorrow night Smith will take 'em in hand again.

"But you notice nights where there is legitimate entertainment on the air and the candidates can't get on why they don't seem to care what happens to the farmer. So it looks to me like the candidates are trying to relieve the farmer of his vote, instead of his debts." (Sept. 19, 1928.)

Farm relief continued to draw comments from Will.

"Just read the farm relief bill. It's just a political version of Einstein's last theory.

"If a farmer could understand it, he certainly would know more than to farm. He would be a professor out here in Harvard. The farmers will die in the poorhouse before the guy that wrote it can even get the Senate to understand it.

"In my dumb way it read like it was all based on doing away with the middleman. That's a great idea and has been tried ever since the snake came between Adam and Eve. He is unnecessary, but he is here yet.

"Then if this did work next year we would have to give relief to the middleman. But it will give 'em something to argue over." (April 15, 1929.)

But now and then something positive would come up.

"The old farmer is getting his relief. I see today where they put high tariff on 'shingles and flax-seed.' Heretofore every time a farmed raised a good crop of 'shingles,' why, he had to compete with Argentine-grown shingles, but with these two new tariffs, why, the old agrarian is sitting pretty. They have taken the 'shingles' off his roof so he can see the Republican viewpoint. He puts a flaxseed poultice on his head and prays that he will never be so unfortunate as to be relieved again." (May 15, 1929.)

But wait! Help is coming.

"I always knew the farmer not only needed relief but he needed some help, and I had become kinder discourage as to him getting it, for there didn't seem any actual way, but this new farm board has come through with an original idea.

"For one hour every day the farmer is to receive assistance over the radio. Different cigarettes have had an hour, and they are all doing pretty well, so they figure an hour's advertising over the radio will just about put agriculture on the level with cigarettes.

"And no farmer could ask more than that." (July 9, 1929.)

And then a friend of Will's came up with a suggestion.

"I like my Injun compatriot Curtis's stand on farm relief. He said: 'Appoint a Congressional committee to study the problem and when they have found about it pass legislation in accordance.' Now who could have thought of a better way to sidetrack anything than to wait till some congressman or senators found out anything about it. That they don't know anything about it in the first place is why they are senators and congressmen." (Aug. 19, 1928.)

Or maybe the president can help.

"Hoover called Congress to aid farm relief and up to now there has been one thousand and twenty-seven bills introduced, one was for farm relief and one thousand twenty-six to aid the members that introduced 'em." (April 17, 1929.)

Well, okay then, maybe an election will help.

"The farmers starve three years out of four but the good year is always election year. It really looks like the Lord was in cahoots with the Republicans, but if He is that would almost make you lose faith in Him. Even up to nominating time this year the farmers wanted relief, now they are so prosperous they would be insulted if you suggested it to 'em.

"Same way four years ago, La Follette was figuring on their support, and he run into a bumper crop. So the only way the Democrats will ever get the farmers' vote is to hold the election in the spring, when they are broke." (Sept. 9, 1928.)

Will took a little trip, but it didn't completely take his mind off the farmers.

"Just flew into this great little Western city (Great Falls, Mont.), last home of Charles M. Russell, the painter. He will live in history as America's most famous cowboy. And his country talks about scenery.

"I flew over the mountains today that make Switzerland look like a prairie dog town. If we could get our mountain farmers to wear feathers in their hats and yodel, we would be as picturesque as Switzerland.

"Maybe the farmer will yodel when they get relieved. They will have time to learn, anyway." (March 31, 1927.)

Speaking of the wide-open spaces:

"The fellows that keep saying big ranches are all done away with ought to see this one, 300,000 acres (near San Simeon, Cal.).

"If this was back East they could call it Delaware, Maryland, Connecticut and Rhode Island, and eight senators and twenty-five congressmen would have to live off it. Out here that much beautiful land don't have to support a thing but wonderful cattle and horses. You can just tell the difference when you look at land that has to support a senator or a white-faced bull." (Oct. 30, 1927.

It always comes back to politics.

"You can always tell when the Senate is getting near a close

– the Boulder Dam bill will come up. Some day somebody with the interest of that bill at heart will bring it up the first day of Congress, and then if some Arizona senator can talk from then to the close, why it will be a record and not just a repetition.

"They knew Coolidge would veto the farm bill.

Well, if they had help this summer, why didn't they have some kind of a compromise bill ready that he would sign. No, sir. There was more politics than relief in that bill." (May 27, 1928.)

This is relief?

"Mr. Hoover's Farm Board has already helped the farmer beyond all expectations. They have told the eight million farm relief societies that infest Washington that they didn't need them and would not do anything through them.

"That's all the aid the farmer has ever needed – just to be relieved of the people who are making a living off of trying to relieve him." (July 23, 1929.)

For once, Will gets serious – he urges the people to help where the government won't:

"Now here is something you mustn't get wrong. The government Saturday passed a bill to appropriate 20 millions as a loan to farmers in the drought area, but it was to be loaned on security.

"Now the man and his family that are hungry down there have no security. If he had any security he wouldn't be hungry. He would have already put it up.

"So, this loan has not relieved the people that the Red Cross has been feeding at all. They have got to go on being fed by the Red Cross.

"So, you towns that have been so slow in raising your quota, because you have been waiting on the government to see what they would do, now you see. So get busy and raise it.

"They have got to be fed till a new crop is raised, and when they raise it, the last one is still in this country. It hasn't been sold yet.

"No town can possibly have an excuse now for not doing their part." (Feb. 16, 1931.)

And then Will issues a report:

"My November message on the 'State of the Nation': The nation never looked like it was facing a worse winter – birds, geese, Democrats and all perishable animals are already huddled up in three or four states down South. We are at peace with the world because the world is waiting to get another gun and get it loaded. Wall Street is in good shape, but Eighth Avenue never was a bad off. The farmers are going into the winter with pretty good radios, but not much feed for their stock." (Dec. 5, 1928.)

And here's a look from another angle:

"We used to always be talking and 'sloganing' about 'back to normalcy.' Well, that's right where we are now, and where we are going to stay, so we might just as well get used to it.

"It's taught us one important fact, that we haven't got as many 'big men' as we thought we had. We used to think every head of a big organization was a 'big man,' and he was as long as everything was running in spite of him, but when old man 'get-back-to-earth' hit us in the jaw, why we didn't have an industry that shrunk like the 'big man' industry did.

"Big men are just like stocks now, they are selling at just what they are worth, no more." (June 4, 1931.)

Never fear – here's the government to the rescue:

"Secretary of Agriculture Wallace is out our way here (California). He has got a tough job. It's by far the toughest job in the Cabinet.

"Sec. of the Navy only has to deal with an admiral, Sec. of the

Army with the generals. Postmaster General with the politicians, but when you deal with the farmer you are dealing with a man who is a dealer himself.

"So if I was Wallace I would say, 'Boys, you all are just too good farmers. You just raise too much. If you just wouldn't be so expert for a few years. It don't do any good to plow under every third row if you are going to raise more on the other two than you did on the three. Your efficiency is driving you to the poor house. So please don't be such good farmers." (May 28, 1934.)

Then Wall Street gets into the act:

"The whole financial structure of Wall Street seems to have fallen on the mere fact that the Federal Reserve Bank raised the amount of interest from 5 to 6 per cent. Any business that can't survive a 1 per cent raise must be skating on mighty thin ice.

"Why, even the poor farmers it took a raise of from 6 to 10 per cent, with another 10 per cent bonus, to get the loan from the banks. It took all that to completely break them, and nobody connected with the government paid any attention.

"But let Wall Street have a nightmare and the whole country has to help get them back in bed again." (Aug. 12, 1929.)

Congress will take care – of itself:

"Did you know that the only bill that has already passed the House and the Senate and been signed by the president is the bill appropriating the salary of the members of this extra session? The farmers can grow whiskers, the orphans can grow up, the tariff can tear out the vitals of the consumers' purse, but the boys there want theirs in advance whether they deliver any relief to anybody else or not." (May 24, 1929.)

The nation's economy wasn't quite so bad a couple of years earlier.

"Mr. Coolidge killed the Farm Relief bill, but the farmers

broke about even. The 'Better Radio' bill passed. Farmers are buying more batteries than they are seeds.

"P.S. – Hurrah! Only four more days of Congressional burglary on the Treasury.

"Another P.S. – I am on my way home to take up any loose divorces that may have accumulated in my municipality during my absence. I am stopping in Arizona, I want to see the state that produces the senators that can talk for three days and nights." (Feb. 27, 1927.)

Iowa farmers come up with a solution:

"The farmers are on strike in Iowa. Instead of selling their stuff for nothing, they just eat it themselves and that saves 'em the expense of hauling it to town. Funny they never thought of that before.

"I have always claimed that if every farmer would eat all that he raised that he would not only get fat himself but farm products might 'probably' go up.

"Course, on account of this not being an economist's idea, it might not work." (Aug. 16, 1932.)

Yes, indeed, Will says to one development.

"Say, you don't rush this Roosevelt into everything that is pulled on him.

"Saturday was refusal day with him (he must have collected a bad stamp). To the farmers' resolution from their convention telling him what to do, he just said 'yeah?' Swope had a plan, and he just said 'yeah?' England's debt commission goes home with nothing but 'yeah?' Wall Street said the dollar must be stabilized. He just said, 'yeah?' They even told him the big bad wolf, Congress, was coming in eight weeks, and he just said 'yeah?'

"It looked like the 'yeah' had it. It takes a lot of 'yeahs' to keep you from being a 'yes' man." (Nov. 5, 1933.)

If it's not one darn thing, it's another.

"I been getting some papers sent to me from the Northwest, and I am telling you, from the pictures, these grasshoppers have laid that country lower than the Farm Board.

"They just swarm onto a place like farmers at a free barbecue, and leave about as little.

"There is one thing to be said for the grasshopper – he has generally operated in the Republican territory. Kansas has been ruined by 'em as often as by their politicians, so that's why the Democrats have never paid the bugs much attention, in fact, kinder urged 'em on. But they never even prayed for anything like this to happen." (July 30, 1931.)

Water is very important to farmers, and to Will:

"Well, Calvin did a mighty fine job of dam dedicating here (Globe, Ariz.) this afternoon. He made a dam good speech favoring dams. Said he didn't want to come at first, but that finally 'President Hoover asked him to come.' He naturally couldn't refuse Mr. Hoover for in a few years they might be opening a Hoover dam and he might want to ask Mr. Hoover to go and dedicate it. He dedicated the bridge to religion, a very beautiful thought and appropriate at this very time, for here is Russia with twice our national resources, three times our size, bending every government energy to throttle all religion. All you have to do is look at the two countries and see whose policy is the best.

"A peculiar thing about the dam that you may not read in your dispatches – the dam is built on the lower side of the Apache Indian reservation, and the water is all to be used by the Pima tribe and the whites. In fact, they moved the Apaches out of the very valley where the water is backed up in, and moved them ten miles up above. The only way the Apaches can ever get any good out of the dam is for somebody to invent a way for water to run uphill. And then they wonder why Apaches are wild.

"One ceremony reminded me of a blindfolded tobacco ad test. Mr. Coolidge and an Apache chief and a Pima chief all took a whiff from the same pipe. The Indians didn't bat an eye, but Calvin coughed over a carload's worth.

"The dam will open up 1,000,000 acres of new land, and there is 1,000,000 farmers starving to death all over our country on farms that's all ready open, so it all depends on where you live, as to how you look at it." (March 4, 1930.)

Chapter 12: Wall Street and Lobbyists

Wait a minute. . .

"We are all in a lather over this Shearer, and the lobbying. If one man with no official connection can change a whole conference, it's not him you want to investigate, it's the guys that he influenced, and it's the same with lobbying in Washington. If we have senators and congressmen there that can't protect themselves against these evil temptations of lobbyists, we don't need to change our lobby, we need to change our representatives.

"Any person that can't spot a propagandist and lobbyist a mile away, must be a person so blind that they still think toupees are deceptive, and can't tell a hotel house detective from a guest." (Sept. 29, 1929.)

Will Rogers was famous for making jokes and kidding people, but one reason he was called a homespun philosopher is because underneath his jokes often was a unique insight into what was wrong with politics. And still is wrong.

His statement above about the influence of lobbyists is as true today as it was in 1929. (And probably will be in 2929, if the voters don't wake up.)

In latter 2011 and early 2012 a series of protests attracted many thousands of persons across the United States, loosely calling themselves "Occupy Wall Street." The protesters set up camps near Wall Street itself, and also in numerous cities across the nation, including Washington, D.C.

As so often happens with this sort of thing, many people joined the movement, not really knowing what they were protesting.

Many of the camps remained in place for weeks and months, eventually leading to confrontation with local police.

At the heart of the protests was the manner in which Wall Street allegedly was to blame for the nation's economic woes, and the fact that the federal government spent a lot of taxpayer money bailing out Wall Street.

" If the goal is to loosen the financiers' grip over the American economy, the folks protesting on K Street are getting closer to bingo. K Street is Washington's famous boulevard of lobbyist influence, the place where money buys politicians to do money's bidding." – Froma Harrop of Creators Syndicate, in Oct. 16, 2011, St. Joseph News-Press.

"If Wall Street paid a tax on every 'game' they run, we would get enough revenue to run the government on." ("Will Says.")

It takes money to make money on Wall Street.

"If you think we are not prosperous and cuckoo both, read these: 'Three hundred thousand dollars for seat on Stock Exchange.' You pay that for a seat where nobody sits down. They stand and yell and sell something they haven't got, and buy something they will never get. You can get on the Curb for forty thousand. All you have to do is make signs to a guy in a window, and try to keep from being run over by a truck.

"In the next column we read 'Kentucky prohibits betting on races.' You can gamble on how high people pay for their bread but you can't bet on how fast a horse will run. We must appear odd to the foreigners." (Nov. 24, 1927.)

It was the calm before the storm in the U.S. economy.

"Big headline in the paper says, 'Three newspaper men arrested in connection with horse-race betting.' In the adjoining column, 'Wall Street stock market reaches another four million; call money is the highest in its history.'

"You don't have to look much further in the paper for humor than that. And we call Latin American governments primitive for allowing lotteries. We only have one rule: If you can build a business up big enough it's respectable.

"Just a sorehead because I didn't have any General Motors." (May 22, 1928.)

But then in 1929 the Stock Market crashed. The very foundations of the nation were shaken. But Will Rogers tried to console the nation.

"Flying from New York, all day just looking down on beautiful lands and prosperous towns, then you read all this sensational collapse of Wall Street.

"What does it mean? Nothing. Why, if the cows of this country failed to come up and get milked one night it would be more of a panic than if Morgan and Lamont had never held a meeting. Why, an old sow and a litter of pigs make more people a living than all the steel and general motor stock combined. Why, the whole 120,000,000 of us are more dependent on the cackling of a hen than if the stock exchange was turned into a night club.

"And New Yorkers call them rubes." (Oct. 25, 1929.)

But a lot of people did take the stock market crash hard.

"I have been in Washington on inauguration day, Claremore on Fourth of July, Dearborn on Edison's Day. But to have been in New York on 'wailing day'! When Wall Street took that tail spin, you had to stand in line to get a window to jump out of, and speculators were selling space for bodies in the East River. If England is supposed by international treaty to protect the Wailing Wall, they will have to come here to do it. The wall runs from the Battery to the Bronx.

"You know there is nothing that hollers as quick and as loud as a gambler. They even blame it on Hoover's fedora hat. Now

they know what the farmer has been up against for eight years."
(Oct. 24, 1929.)

There was no easy solution.

"Sure must be a great consolation to the poor people who lost their stock in the late crash to know that it has fallen in the hands of Mr. Rockefeller, who will take care of it and see that it has a good home and never be allowed to wander around unprotected again.

"There is one rule that works in every calamity. Be it pestilence, war or famine, the rich get richer and the poor get poorer. The poor even help arrange it. But it's just as Mr. Brisbane and I have been constantly telling you, 'Don't gamble'; take all your savings and buy some good stock, and hold it till it goes up, then sell it.

"If it don't go up, don't buy it." (Oct. 31, 1929.)

When in doubt, blame it on the stock market crash.

"Mr. Hoover has had all the financiers of the country gathered and made 'em sign a pledge to spend some money for the general prosperity of the country. So next week he is really going into big business. He is calling the coaches of the various football teams together and get them to promise to build bigger grandstands, make longer trips and pay more for promising high school talent.

"That's what's the matter with this country. It's not Wall Street, it's not the Senate, it's just that a lot of cheap colleges won't go out and spend the dough. Bigger grandstands! Look at Chicago with Soldiers Field, with Dempsey and Tunney, Army and Navy and California and Notre Dame! Why, that's brought 'em more publicity than Al Capone and machine guns combined." (Nov. 29, 1929.)

And then Will took it personally:

"Been having a lot of trouble here lately getting some alfalfa to grow on my little patch of ground.

"One span of gray mules don't look as well as they ought to, according to what they are eating.

"I never missed a polo ball as much in my life as I did last Sunday. Seen a couple of mighty poor movies here lately.

"But, as soon as the market picks up, you watch these mules go, and this grass grow and pictures improve.

"I tell you, it's the stock market crash last fall that did it." (July 15, 1930.)

But is the stock market really that crucial?

"Mr. Whitney, the man in charge of all the 'faro and roulette tables' of the New York Stock Exchange, throwed a scare into Mr. Hoover and some congressmen yesterday by telling 'em if they stopped speculators selling something 'they haven't got' – well, it would stop the Stock Exchange, and people with stocks would have to sell 'em like folks with horses, or cows, of wheat, for just what they are worth.

"Now you can just imagine the terrible consequences of that exchange being closed. Why, it would be terrible!

"At least 115,000,000 out of the 120,000,000 would put on a celebration that would make Armistice Day look like a wake." (Feb. 25, 1932.)

Eventually, the stock disaster began to steady somewhat.

"All I know is just what I read in want ads. I see where they say Wall Street is coming back. Yep, coming back for more. They figure people about had time to save up another little dab. That's one good thing about the rascals though, they always give you warning when they are coming.

"There ought to be some way figured out just what it takes to support that whole gang (in the manner in which they are accustomed) then charge everybody in the U.S. so much and deduct it from their salary. That would eliminate all speculation, and everybody would know just where they stood." (Nov. 21, 1930.)

Maybe there is life after Wall Street.

"After Wall Street had been dead for a couple of years and everybody that had so generously contributed to the funeral was just about to go to work and forget about it, why now the United States Senate, that investigates everything after it's dead, is going to dig up the body and hold an autopsy. They will find out exactly what everyone else already knows, 'deceased died from overgorging while the gorging was gorgeous.'" (April 11, 1932.)

But the Senate proceeds anyhow.

"Today's news featured two items in the same column 'Monte Carlo fails to pay dividend for first time' and 'Wall Street investigation still carried on.'

"Senate has been investigating Wall Street for ten days and all they have found out is that the street is located in the sharp end of New York City, that not only the traders but the street itself is short, that neither end don't lead anywhere." (April 19, 1932.)

The beat goes on.

"Mr. Roosevelt is the only man who can raise the stock market without putting up any money.

"The market not only operates on O.P.M. (other people's money) but O.P.R. (other people's rumors).

"A war in Europe would mean nothing to the stock market (provided it actually happened) but let a rumor get out that Mr. Ford was building a six-door sedan or that the present government was going to recognize Tammany Hall, or that Bernard Baruch was growing a beard – any of these rumors and wheat would jump 10 points, American Can 8, and American T. & T. 9.

"So the only thing can break the stock market is a fact." (Oct. 24, 1933.)

Are lobbyists really necessary? Do they do any good?

"It all boils down to a matter of perspective. One city official explains, 'Whether you think lobbyists are good or evil depends on whose ox is being gored." – Danny Tyree of Cagle Syndicate in the Nov. 14, 2011, St. Joseph News-Press.

"A lobbyist is a person that is supposed to help a politician make up his mind – not only help him but pay him." ("Will Says.")

"Landing in Newark from Washington today, the pilot put us in the back end of the plane, so it would keep her tail down when the wheels hit the deep snow.

"Give you an idea how many thousand men clearing the streets in New York, they have misplaced 51 thousand and can't find 'em.

"Seven below zero in Washington this morning and snow a foot deep. Lobbyists standing frozen to death outside of congressmen's homes. A lobbyist has nothing to keep him warm but his brief case." (Feb. 28, 1934.)

"California had a bill to investigate lobbying, and the lobbyists bought off all the votes and they can't even find the bill now. Putting a lobbyist out of business is like a hired man trying to fire his boss." (April 3, 1935.)

The Great Depression rocked the entire nation for too long. But, as usually happens in the financial world, another cycle turned over and things began to get better again.

"It's surprising how little money we can get along on. Let the banks never open. Let scrip never come. Just everybody keep on trusting everybody else.

"Why, it's such a novelty to find that somebody will trust you that it's changed our whole feeling toward human nature. Why, never was our country so united, never was a country so tickled with their poverty.

"For three years we have had nothing but 'America is fundamentally sound.' It should have been 'America is fundamentally cuckoo.'

"The worse off we get the louder we laugh, which is a great thing. And every American international banker ought to have printed on his office door 'Alive today by the grace of a nation that has a sense of humor.'" (March 8, 1933.)

Well, we can always investigate something.

"New York Stock Exchange is having their own investigation. They are investigating fourteen different stocks that have been acting so funny that Wall Street itself didn't know what they were doing. In other words you can fool the public, but you mustn't fool the members of the lodge.

"The high income tax come pretty near passing Thursday in the Senate. Only lacked about six votes. So it won't be long now. Well, there is millions and millions that are not making it, that would be glad to give up 99 per cent if you would let 'em earn a hundred thousand or more." (April 6, 1934.)

"Senate passed the bill to regulate Wall Street. The government is going to put traffic lights on it. It's always been a hit and run street.

"The red light tells you you better stop and wait before buying, the green light tells you that you are a sucker anyhow and you might just as well go ahead. The yellow light means, put up no more margins, let 'em sell you out." (May 13, 1934.)

There are those who say playing the stock market is a form of gambling, at least for those who are not experts.

"Every nation must have its legalized form of gambling.

We have our Wall Street. Mexico gives you a more even break. They have 'roulette,' also a percentage of your losings go to the government. They are a primitive race. They put government above broker.

"Folks will take a chance. Old Noah gambled on not getting the 'foot and mouth' disease in there with all those animals, and old King Solomon bet a hundred women he wouldn't pay 'em alimony and won his bet. 'Viva la Mexico.'" (March 16, 1930.)

As New York City goes, so goes. . .

"Say, these New York weather fellows deliver the goods. They advertised in all the papers yesterday that they had another storm in rehearsal, that they would be ready to produce one that would be a bigger production than the last one, and by gosh I believe it looks tonight like the boys are going to make good.

"Clark Gable is back here appearing on the stage and I am here trying to help keep the women off him.

"The big brokers of Wall Street are all moving down to Washington, for all their big clients are on the stand there all the time. They are putting tickers in the investigating rooms now." (Feb. 25, 1934.)

Sometimes Will Rogers couldn't find an especially newsy topic for the day.

"They say the air mail will be flying commercially soon.

"They say Congress votes on greenbacks for bonus money now.

"The say Dillinger is headed West (but I bet you not to Tucson, Ariz.)

"They say the president is going to appoint a warden for Wall Street.

"All these don't mean a thing in the papers today. But when

Rabbit Maranville breaks a leg right at the opening of the season that constitutes America's greatest crisis." (March 29, 1934.)

President Franklin D. Roosevelt had introduced what he called the New Deal for the nation. So it was up to Will Rogers to explain what that meant.

"You hear people say, 'What is this New Deal, anyhow?'

"Well, there was a headline today that explains it.

"'Wall Street Anxiously Awaits the President's Message.'

"Well, in the 'Old Deal' it was the president that was anxiously waiting till Wall Street sent him the message to read." (Jan. 3, 1935.)

Chapter 13: Elections and Crime

That don't mean the same thing...

"In most places it's awful hard to get folks to go and register to vote, but out here in Los Angeles where we do everything 'big' why each qualified voter is allowed to register himself and ten dead friends. If he hasn't got ten dead friends, why he is allowed to pick out ten live ones, just so they don't live in this state.

"The Republicans are kicking on this arrangement, as they claim that system of registration gives the Democrats the best of it, as very few Republicans have ten friends.

"You ought to come out here some time. We do have the most fun." (Oct. 17, 1934.)

Will Rogers had a few other comments about elections:

"In this country people don't vote for, they vote against."

"The short memories of American voters is what keeps our politicians in office."

"Imagine a man in public office that everybody knew where he stood. We wouldn't call him a statesman, we would call him a curiosity."

For some reason or other, Will seemed to like this term "statesman."

"Well, this day after election many a good man will find that he has been replaced because he failed to bring in enough government loot from Washington.

"Did you ever figure what constitutes our modern 'representative'? The one that can bring home the new federal post office, even if they wasn't using the old one; federal aid for roads that nobody may ever drive on, and a government dam.

"The height of statesmanship is to come home with a dam, even if you got nowhere to put it. Just raid the national treasury enough and you will soon be referred to as a 'statesman.'" (Nov. 4, 1930.)

But even these things called elections will pass in due time.

"There is only one redeeming thing about this whole election. It will be over at sundown, and let everybody pray that it's not a tie, for we couldn't go through with this thing again.

"And, when the votes are counted, let everybody, including the candidates, get into a good humor as quick as they got into a bad one.

"Both gangs have been bad sports, so see if at least one can't redeem themselves by offering no alibis, but cooperate with the winner, for no matter which one it is the poor fellow is going to need it.

"So cheer up. Let's all be friends again. One of the evils of democracy is you have to put up with the man you elect whether you want him or not. That's why we call it democracy." (Nov. 7, 1932.)

Will Rogers had a special attachment to election day.

"I was born on Nov. 4, which is election day. . . My birthday has made more men and sent more back to honest work than any other days in the year."

Sometimes an election can get a little out of hand.

"As a life member of the Red Cross we are rushing doctors and nurses to Chicago with all speed to have them there when the bombing starts Tuesday morning. We are establishing first-aid stations just about where we figure the voting booths will be blown up.

"I am covering the Chicago election for the Nicaraguan press. As we are putting on their election for them in October they are anxious to learn what it will be like. The roads away down here are packed with refugees leaving Chicago." (April 8, 1928.)

"So much money is being spent on the campaigns that I doubt if either man, as good as they are, are worth what it will cost to elect them."

"Yesterday our municipal election ran true to political form [in Beverly Hills, Cal.]. The sewer was defeated, but the councilmen got in.

"In our big murder case out here the fellow they are trying for a double come pretty near being elected to the office of judge. Looks like if he had bumped off three instead of two he would have been elected." (June 3, 1931.)

"We don't seem to be able to even check crime. Why not legalize it and put a heavy tax on it. Make the tax for robbery so high that a bandit couldn't afford to rob anyone unless he had a lot of dough. We have taxed other industries out of business, it might work here."

Maybe taxation on crime would work, because sometimes it seems that the pardon and parole system leaves a lot to be desired.

"In a Los Angeles bank robbery last week, due to the bravery of a bank official and the efficiency of the police, two robbers were killed. They caught all the rest. I think it was four captured.

"Well, I wish you read the crime and jail records of all those six men. They had been pardoned or paroled from every institution in the state at least once a month for the last fifteen years.

"Their records read like they had played a series of one-night stands in each jail. They wasn't prisoners. They were traveling men, making hotels out of jails, and that's not an unusual case in any state.

"Pardoning has been one industry that hasn't been hit by depression. When have you read anywhere of a crime being committed by an amateur?" (Aug. 31, 1932.)

A little more about amateurs:

"There must not be such a thing in this country as what you would call an 'amateur crook.' Every person that is caught in some terrible crime you find where he has been 'paroled, pardoned and pampered' by every jail or insane asylum in the country. Some of these criminals' records and the places they have been freed from, it sounds like the tour of a 'one-night theatrical troupe.'

"It must be awfully monotonous belonging to one of these state pardon boards. There is days and nights when they just have to sit around waiting for new criminals to be caught so they can pardon 'em." (Oct. 18, 1934.)

Well, then, it's on to Chicago:

"Playing Chicago tomorrow night, perhaps. Hope I reach the stage before the machine gun bullets lay me low. I want to go with my chaps on. Everybody in America has been good to me and I love you all, even critics and congressmen." (Nov. 22, 1926.)

"The government has finally been able to arrange an 'armistice' with Al Capone.

"He is to go to jail 'in person' for two years (which term he named himself). His lieutenants are to carry on his business and deliver the receipts to him at the jail every day.

"In return the government is to feed, clothe and protect him from harm and release him just about the time business turns the corner.

"The government is remodeling Leavenworth now for him." (June 18, 1931.)

If Chicago doesn't suit your taste, let's try Oklahoma.

"You can't beat Oklahoma for originality.

"Guess you read about the outlaws with a big truck (with a winch attachment) on it backed up to the bank to kidnap the safe. Everybody in town came down to see the show.

"Due to the outlaws having done no physical work in so long they wasn't stout enough to load it. But they notified the bank that they will be back right away and that the bank is to have s smaller safe.

"The future of bank robberies is to arrange some way to charge admission. So many people seeing robberies free is what's killing the business." (June 20, 1934.)

If the crime business is slow in the U.S., let's see what is going on in England (this also sounds like some things going on in the U.S. in 2012):

"Well, the conference didn't do anything today as usual, but there was a famous case being tried where a fellow had swindled through fake stock transactions the people out of ten million dollars. They just give him fourteen years so fast that it took all the Americans' breath away and all they have talked about today is English justice compared to ours. It's the consensus of opinion of all of them here that if it had been at home he would have gone into vaudeville or the Senate.

"None of the habus corpusing and suspended sentences or appealing when you commit a crime over here. You just wake up surrounded by a small space. Our delegation ought to be over here studying British justice. Our battleships are not harming us near as much as court delays, corruption and shyster lawyers." (Jan. 24, 1930.)

Back to good old American crime in California:

"This murderer out here, Hickman, confessed, so that means

a long-drawn-out trial. It's going to be a fight to a finish between the alienists and the photographers.

"American murder procedure is about as follows: Foul enough to commit a crime, dumb enough to get caught, smart enough to prove you was crazy when you committed it and fortunate enough to show you was too sane to hang." (Jan. 23, 1928.)

Well, when you talk about crime, it's hard to ignore Chicago.

"Just passed thru Chicago. It's not a boast, it's an achievement. That's a big city. It's growing, by heaps and mounds. The snow was so deep today the crooks could only hit a tall man. To try and diminish crime they laid off six hundred cops.

"Chicago has no tax money. All their influential men are engaged in tax exempt occupations. What they got to do is to tax murder. Put such a stiff tax on it that only the higher class gangsters can afford it. It's the riff raff that makes any business disreputable." (Jan. 9, 1930.)

Well, Chicago is not the only place with crime.

"Went over to New York today. See where Police Commissioner Whalen appointed a crime commission of twenty to help him keep a list of the crimes. If they hear of any that he don't, why they report them to him. Then at the end of the year the one that has heard about the most crimes gets the prize." (May 16, 1929.)

Or how about Philadelphia?

"This is Al Capone that is supposed to be field marshal on Chicago's western front. Well in Miami and Chicago and all the other cities he has been received by the mayor, Chamber of Commerce and Daughters of Various Revolutions, but he blew into our little City of Brotherly Love here yesterday and before his valet could unpack his machine gun why he had been sentenced to a year in jail for wearing pistols instead of a vest. That's one of the worst blows against our new aristocracy we have had." (May 17, 1929.)

Oh, well, there's always good old Chicago.

"Here is something Chicago ought to put on billboards and announce to the world.

"No innocent man has been murdered here since the World's Fair in '93.

"And also, rival gangs do not murder each other. They are killed by members of their own gang for 'holding out' and at double-crossing.

"A 'square' gangster can die in this town of old age, and an innocent citizen to be shot here, would have to commit suicide.

"I tell you this system has a lot of merit to it. Wouldn't it be great if bankers 'bumped off' the crooked ones." (June 26, 1930.)

Maybe not in Chicago, but sometimes in other places people who do bad things end up in prison.

"Atlanta Prison is kicking because Miss Willebrandt has been sending in government spies disguised as prisoners to see how the place is run. Now I have been getting lots of letters from friends in there. Every one of them rates it the best jail they were ever in. They all say the warden could go out on his own and open up an independent jail and have it filled in no time with men that appreciate the better type of jails. They don't kick on associating with bankers, and even politicians, but don't want the same jail with spies.

"Now I know Mabel, and I know my friends in there, and I just want to get it settled if I can. It will just ruin that jail, cause every one of them write me, if it's kept up, they would never go back to that jail again. So do what you can for 'em, Mabel." (March 14, 1929.)

Elections are not necessarily related in any way to criminal conduct, it says here. But sometimes some funny things happen on the way to the voting booth.

"News of the day about Tuesday's elections: Smith carried New York through force of habit. Vare carried Philadelphia through something. It may not have been just habit alone. Cleveland, Ohio, admitted they needed a mayor and New Mexico here voted that if any man couldn't get it in two years in this state that there was no use giving him four.

"Kentucky decided it was all right for the state to have some of the money bet on horse races, that the profit should not all go to the bookmakers." (Nov. 9, 1927.)

Will Rogers was himself a Democrat, but sometimes he wondered about the party.

"Hurrah for Texas for taking the comedy away from Oklahoma!

"I have heard of a man being made a Democrat by persuasion, perculiarity of mind mostly by purchase. But the great state of Texas is the first one to make a man (or his two-legged equivalent) a Democrat by act of Legislature. They passed a bill saying 'if you are a Democrat, you have to stay a Democrat. You can't vote one way one election and one way the next. If you are a man that changes your mind, you are not a Democrat.

"It don't say anything about the Republicans. They can go over to the Democrats without committing bigamy.

"Now here is a tip to my good friend Dan Moody, the governor. When a child is born of what is suspected of Democratic parentage, brand it with the letter 'D' on the left hip. Then at the election time just run 'em through the chute and tally 'em." (March 12, 1929.)

Will gets so put out with the Democrats that he tries to get rid of them:

"FOR SALE – Would like to sell, trade, dispose of or give away to right parties franchise of what is humorously known as Democratic Party. Said franchise calls for license to enter in national elections; said right of franchise is supposed to be used every four years, but if intelligent parties had it they would let various elections go by default when understood they had no chance.

"If in right hands and only used in times when it had an 'issue' or when Republican Party had split, think it could be made to pay, but present owners have absolutely no business with it. Under present management they have killed off more good men than grade crossings have." (Nov. 7, 1929.)

It didn't take long for Will to get some offers for the Democrats.

"Offers pouring in all day for the purchase of the Democrats. All want the title, but no one wants any of the cast.

"I bet preachers are looking for a new act more than I am after election. It will take them months to get their minds back on religion. Nobody knows yet who is governor in this state (New York). There is a Jewish fellow running, and if he gets it and makes a good governor for four terms, why, the religious issue won't come up again for president till 1936.

"Smith carried all the Democratic states he didn't go into, and Hoover had a cinch in all the Republican ones he didn't speak in. I believe a dumb candidate could have beat 'em both." (Nov. 8, 1929.)

Politicians talk about "restoring confidence" in the nation, so Will Rogers decides to try his hand at it:

"Been looking to see what I could do toward 'restoring confidence' and discovered the following facts:

"Confidence hasn't left the country; confidence has just got wise, and the guys that it got wise to are wondering where it has gone.

"Railroad men of the country held a meeting in Washington and decided to put on more bus lines.

"Newspapers headline the fact that 19 were killed in Mexico election day, and it should be head-lined, for it is astonishing, astonishing to us, for we can bump off that many electing an alderman in Chicago, or any of our big cities.

"Mexico has got a long way to be before they reach our state of civilization." (Nov. 20, 1929.)

When things seem confused, the best thing to do is to name a committee to look into the problem.

"President Hoover is about finished appointing the committee that is to bring milk and honey to the famished agrarian. It looks like an awfully simple problem they have to solve. All they have to do is get the farmer more money for his wheat, corn and cotton without raising the price to the man that buys it.

"The committee will meet and then appoint subcommittees, and the subcommittees will appoint an investigating committee, and just before the next presidential election the investigating committee will turn in a report: 'After due examination we find the farmer really in need of succor and we advise making one out of him at the coming election.'" (June 30, 1929.)

Maybe politicians would be better off if they got right to the point, Will suggests.

"Seemed like old times last night to hear Mr. Coolidge on the radio, especially when he pleaded for 'a continuation of Republican blessings.'

"He said what we needed in office was 'officeholders,' men that were used to holding office. He said it was no time to break in new talent.

"Compare that campaign plea with the one of my friend's Governor Beulow of South Dakota, who is out for the Senate and who says, 'There is no issue in this election; the other fellow has got a job and I want it.'

"Such honesty must come from a Democrat. It does, and it should be rewarded at the polls." (Oct. 31, 1930.)

In year 2012 there are likely to be a number of "lame duck" members of the U.S. Congress, or those who will serve out a few months after the November election results show they will not serve another term. Will Rogers was aware of some like that.

"The Senate is trying to get the Wickersham committee to tell them where they got all their dope from. What the Senate really ought to ask 'em is, where did you get your opinions from after you had received all your dope?

"The lame duck bill comes up this week. A lame duck is a man that didn't bring home enough 'loot' from the National Treasury to warrant his re-election, but they let him stay there thirteen months longer to see if he won't reform and bring home at least a new postoffice building, or enough to widen Polecat Creek." (Feb. 23, 1931.)

Will hears that small towns are disappearing.

"Just reading these late census reports and it shows that the small town is passing. We not only ought to regret it, we ought to do something to remedy it. It was the incubator that hatched all our big men, and that's why we haven't got as many big men today as we used to have.

"Start to have a presidential election nowadays and we have to postpone it, neither side has got anybody big enough to run. Take every small-town-raised big man out of business and you would have nobody left running it but vice presidents.

"You can kid about the old rubes that sat around the cracker barrel, spit in the stove, and fixed the nation, but they were all doing their own thinking. They didn't have their minds made up by some propagandist speaker at the 'Get Nowhere' Luncheon Club.

"Yours for more small town rubes." (April 16, 1930.)

Finally Will observes election results he likes.

"This country is coming back.

"The best indication was old Kentucky. She disposed of sixteen at Tuesday's elections. That's a mighty good showing on what's called an off election year, and when you consider that they needn't have voted at all, for prohibition had already been repealed by thirty-six states.

"Old Kentucky has a law which gives the doctors the benefit of the doubt. They won't count votes or bodies till the next day.

"Clubs were wielded and heads were disorganized in New York, too. This is all a good omen. It shows we are getting out of our effeminate period of voting where you do nothing but vote.

"Led by the spirit of old Kentucky we are returning to American principles. All but the Carolinas." (Nov. 9, 1933.)

Will notes an interesting election result in England.

"The best in conspicuous humor of the week comes out of Washington, as usual. The British ambassador says no more liquor will be shipped in while he is there. Now here is the catch. He didn't say this until after his side had lost the election at home, which means that he will soon be out of a job embassing. By declaring this he gets the next one in bad by having set a precedent and incidentally not being entirely destitute of sustenance during the remainder of his short stay because there is enough on hand by economizing to last.

"Diplomacy is a great thing if it wasn't transparent." (June 6, 1929.)

Chapter 14: Government and Taxes

Well, you can't have one without. . .

"See where the Senate is to start debate on the tariff bill and Mr. Reed Smoot injected the first humorous angle to it by demanding a resolution which would limit the debate to nothing but the subject of the tariff.

"Ha! Ha! It will start with a discussion for a 3 per cent ad valorem duty on imported bird-seed. Taking the affirmative side will be Tom Heflin, with a birds-eye view of the mistake of allowing the Vatican more territory and a motion to prevent Al Smith from building the highest building in NewYork. Then will be a two weeks' discussion on prohibition, followed by ten days of Arizona senators denouncing the Boulder Dam, and by Christmas you won't know whether the birds got any seed or not." (Sept. 2, 1929.)

Sometimes even Will Rogers thought taxes were no laughing matter.

"This is income tax paying day. There is going to be no attempt at humor, for it would be mighty forced. No two can agree on what is deductible. When it's made out you don't know if you are crook or martyr. It's made more liars of the American people than golf, and this is a good time to bring up again the sales tax. Why don't we have it? Then when a thing is bought and paid for you know the government got their tax for it. States have gasoline tax and they collect it without any trouble, and we don't notice it.

"By the way, did you charge off money given to the Democratic campaign? You could, it's a legitimate charity, not organized but a charity nevertheless." (March 15, 1929.)

And when Congress tries to tax somebody, their lobbyists show up in force.

"Every time Congress starts to tax some particular industry, it rushes down with its main men and they scare 'em out of it. About the only way I see for 'em to do, so it would be fair to everybody, would be for Congress to go into secret session, allow no telephones, no telegrams, no visitors, so no outside lobbyists can get at 'em, then tax everything they want to, and should tax, then announce, 'Boys, it's all over; there is no use shooting at us now.'

"As it is now, we are taxing everybody without a lobby." (Feb. 29, 1932.)

Members of Congress seem to have a different way of looking at things, according to Will.

"The Senate slept on the tax bill over the weekend. But the birds that are going to have to pay it didn't sleep any.

"Some senators say that no man should be allowed to earn over $75,000 a year. They forget that a man that earns that much, or more, works for a different kind of an employer from the one senators work for.

"Suppose you got $100,000 a year for working for a firm and you spent $200,000,000 of their money that you didn't have and you didn't know where you was going to get it, how long would you be working for that firm?" (May 16, 1932.)

Meanwhile, the wheels in Washington keep spinning (too often in circles). But a refreshing thing brightened things there.

"Say, did you read the speeches of those high school kids in that final debating in Washington? Sounded like the only first-class oratory that had been pulled in Washington in years. "They give 'em an unprepared subject to talk on, and they were all marvelous. We got to quit knocking these young folks. They may be raising Cain, but by golly, they are smart.

"A young girl, second cousin of mine, from Muskogee, Okla., was given the subject 'harbeas corpus' to speak on. Why, half of us don't know if it's a disease or a new tooth paste, or a radio announcer's real name." (May 25, 1930.)

Do you sometimes feel as if our government doesn't do anything for us?

"If at times you feel your government is not interested in you, you are all wrong. Why, every ten years they send around to see if you are still living and why. They take your name and address and if anything shows up during the next ten years they will notify you.

"Knowing how many of us there is don't mean a thing. Censuses are just for Chambers of Commerce oratorical purposes. The new census will give California six new congressmen. Now if you can call that adding to human welfare you are an optimist.

"Yours for less census and more senses and cents." (April 17, 1930.)

Will has some comments about government in general.

"The money we spend on government. And it's not a bit better government than we got for one-thirds the money two years ago."

"Never blame a legislative body for not doing something. When they do nothing, they don't hurt anybody. It's when they do something is when they get dangerous."

"Nothing will upset a state economic condition like a

legislature. It's better to have termites in your house than the legislature."

Does this sound familiar? Will Rogers questions why the president of the United States does some of the things he does.

"This fellow Roosevelt can close banks, he can tell industry how much to pay and how many hours to work, he can hold back the sun, he can evaporate the water, but when he demands that a postmaster has to be able to read, that's carrying dictatorship too far.

"When he takes the postmasters out of politics he is monkeying with the very fundamentals of American political parties. How is the army going to fight if they don't get any of the loot?

"I tell you this suggestion of his is bordering on treason. The idea of a postmaster being able to read. It looks like an undemocratic move to favor the college man. I tell you he will ruin the Democratic party. We mustn't let him get away with it." (July 13, 1933.)

It wasn't limited to postmasters.

"The president signed another loan bill. This one for only $125,000,000 for land banks. Then last week $2,000,000,000. You can tell this is an election year from the way these appropriation bills are passing. It will take the taxpayers fifty years to pay for the votes in this election.

"Our only solution of relief seems to be to fix it so people who are in a hole through borrowing can borrow some more. Borrowing, that's what's the matter with the world today. If no individual or country could borrow a dime for five years that would be the greatest five-year plan ever invented." (Jan. 25, 1932.)

The president must have some close advisers.

"Say, that list of new Cabinet members sent everybody

scurrying through Who's Who Almanac and the United States finger print department trying to find out who they were.

"The forgotten man has been found, and there was nine of 'em and a woman.

"So we open March 4th with the 'unknown Cabinet.' The rogues gallery photographs show us that three of 'em escaped from the Senate. That's like going to the old man's home to get an athlete.

"But I believe they are going to be all right. They all got their reputations to make, which is better than feeling that they have one already made." (Feb. 23, 1933.)

The cost of government keeps going up.

"Mr. Calvin Coolidge had a mighty instructive article on finances in last week's Sat-Eve-Post.

"We got a long-sighted government. When everybody has more money they cut the taxes, and when they're broke they raise 'em. That's statesmanship of the highest order.

"The reason there wasn't much unemployment in the last ten years preceding '29 was every man that was out of a job went to work for the government – state or city.

"It costs ten times more to govern us than it used to, and we are not governed one-tenth as good." (March 27, 1932.)

Along comes a new kind of mail – who's going to handle it?

"This air mail thing – wish they would get them all kinder calmed down over it.

"Everybody is so heated up over it till they can't see the other fellow's side, or any other side, but theirs.

"No use talking about what the government shouldn't have done. It's done done. No use saying 'the government can't to this, and they can't do that.' Say, you would be surprised at the things the government can do.

"The Army may not be the one to carry the mails. I don't think so, but I am not going to go to blows with anybody over it. After all, it's the government's mail and the government's Army. They can do what they want to do with it.

"This thing is not going to be settled according to any one man's wishes, so they'd just as well cool off and start compromising now." (March 18, 1933.)

"As bad as we sometimes think our government is run, it is the best run I ever saw."

Well, if you want something to talk about, there are always taxes.

"The idea that a tax on something keeps anybody from buying it is a lot of 'hooey.' They put it on gasoline all over the country and it hasn't kept a soul at home a single night or day. You could put a dollar a gallon on and still a pedestrian couldn't cross the street with safety without armor."

"Put a good tax on beer and that would take care of the unemployment fund."

"It's a great country but you can't live in it for nothing."

"Comedians haven't improved. Nothing has improved but taxes."

"I see a good deal of talk from Washington about lowering taxes. I hope they do get 'em down enough so people can afford to pay 'em."

Will Rogers often took swipes at Congress, but once in a while he complimented those elected men and women.

"I tell you things never was looking better. And Congress! I want to go on record as giving those rascals a world of credit. They have reformed and they look like they are sorry for what they have done for years.

"Nowadays Mr. Roosevelt just makes a little list of things

every morning that he wants them to do (kinder like a housewife's menu list), and for the first time in their lives they are acting like United States citizens and not like United States senators or congressmen.

"There has never been anything radically wrong with our lawmakers only they thought they were thinking. Now we got a man to do their thinking for 'em, and the whole country is better off." (March 17, 1933.)

Whew. It's not often Will said things like that. But then he used famous pilot Charles Lindbergh to clarify the government worker's role.

"Glad to see Lindbergh's kinder settling down since his engagement. He only flew from Kansas City to Wichita yesterday. Certainly going back in his flying, and say, this marriage has made him hustle out and get him a job. He is working for the government 'on days when he has nothing else to do and is flying over Washington.' But after all, that's not an odd arrangement, for everybody that works for the government 'just works for it when they have nothing else to do.' But this is the first time that's ever been stipulated in a contract.

"New York gave Washington a great birthday today. If he had been here it would have reminded him of Valley Forge." (Feb. 22, 1929.)

And speaking of taxes, Will liked to do that:

"The good old days with most of us was when we didn't earn enough to pay an income tax."

" People want just taxes more than they want lower taxes. They want to know that every man is paying proportionate share according to his wealth."

"When a party can't think of anything else they always fall back on lower taxes. It has a magic sound to a voter just like

Fairyland is spoken of and dreamed of by children. But no child has ever seen it. Neither has any voter ever lived to see the day when his taxes were lowered."

But let's go back to government.

"Just messing around seeing some of our wonderful country. Here in Santa Fe (New Mexico), the oldest town in America, the tourists say, 'Oh, aren't the people quaint and unique! I wonder what they do and think about.'

"Well, today they are voting on the same thing New York state is – whether to keep a governor two years or four. So, wherever there is politics, people have the same worries. I think a good, honest governor should get four years and the others life.

"As we become more enlightened we will extinguish our office seekers every two years." (Nov. 8, 1927.)

On a more serious note, Will Rogers often raised funds for needy people, especially after some disaster like a flood, tornado or earthquake. He was quick to point out what common citizens can accomplish – when residents of a small town demanded food for their families.

"We got a powerful government, brainy men, great organizations, many commissions, but it took a little band of five hundred simple country people (who had no idea they were doing anything historical) to come to a country town store and demand food for their wives and children, they hit the hearts of the American people, more than all your senatorial pleas, and government investigations.

"Paul Revere just woke up Concord. These birds woke up America.

"I don't want to discourage Mr. Mellon and his carefully balanced budget, but you let this country get hungry and they are going to eat, no matter what happens to budgets, income taxes or Wall Street values.

"Washington mustn't forget who rules when it comes to showdown." (Jan. 6, 1931.)

There is no getting away from taxes.

"We have it on the best of our information that taxes will be relieved, but not until after your death."

"Congress has passed the big inheritance tax. That gets you when you're gone. I think it's a good law. You had had the use of the money during your lifetime, so turn it over to the government and they can do some darn fool things with it. Maybe as foolish as the children of the deceased would. It's only one generation from a pick handle to a putter and one more from a tuxedo to a tramp."

"The government floated an eight hundred million dollar loan the other day and Al Capone took most of it himself. There is the guy that should be secretary of the treasury. Just turn him over the country and split the profits with him.

"I see by today's statistics of what the soldiers have done with their late bonus money that a big item is second-hand cars. Sorry to hear that. We haven't got twenty men in America that are well off to support one." (June 8, 1931.)

"Just passed through Jefferson City, Mo., the home of the state prison and the state capitol. The worst in the state is sent there. The sheriff was on our train and he had two men who had escaped, and he was taking them back to the Legislature." (Feb. 23, 1928.)

Today there is much concern about the federal debt. Will Rogers also worried about that.

"Mr. Mellon has skimped and saved and got together $185,000,000 over and above what Congress nicked him for.

Now they are all arguing over what to do with it, but nobody has ever suggested applying it on our national debt, which is over $30,000,000,000.

"Sixty per cent of all our taxes go toward interest on our various debts, national, state, town and county. But they will take this little dab and try to buy some party voters with it in the way of lower taxes. You wouldn't see Mellon doing that if it applied to his personal affairs. He would get his debt paid off before he started handing anybody anything, but that's just why so many of our individuals are so much richer than our government." (July 3, 1929.)

Even when Will Rogers took a trip overseas, he was concerned with taxes at home.

"What are they doing over home about the sales tax?

"That's the best and most equitable tax there is. The gasoline tax, which is nothing but a sales tax, has proven painless, productive and punitive.

"Now, if a tax on gasoline keeps up all the roads why wouldn't a tax on light wines and beers keep up the House of Representatives, one on Coca-Cola and Jamaican ginger and Camembert cheese keep up the Senate, White Rock and cracked ice the state legislatures, and so on on everything that we have to have or hire and make each stay within the budget.

"For instance, if people wasn't drinking much beer, we wouldn't have many congressmen; if toothpaste and facial creams had a slump, why cut the president's salary in proportion.

"It looks like a good scheme from over here." (Jan. 5, 1932.)

Will even compared the mail system in England with ours:

"Just like to show you what our cousins are doing in the way of toting the mail.

"'London. March 16. The British postoffice showed a profit

at the end of this fiscal year of seventy million dollars. Last year $57,000,000 postoffice profits were applied to the reduction of taxes.'

"We lost 150 million a year. Who's looney now?

"They also run the telephone and telegraph, so when you say, 'a government can't run a business,' you mean our government can't run it.

"So don't forget to always to put that word 'our' in there.

"Jim, this is no reflection on you and your P.O. gang. It's on our lawmakers who won't charge for a letter, paper or crate of eggs what it costs to carry it, be it by plane, boat, train or mule, and charge accordingly." (May 20, 1933.)

Meanwhile, the government comes up with another one.

"Just when the country was doing all it could to economize in government why along comes a law and says, 'Every time your state gets so many thousand new population, they must all throw in and hire another representative in their state for Congress.'

"Well, California foolishly grew, and now they got to pay for it. A dozen unemployed must be sent to Congress by the taxpayers. Well, California is split wide in two, the north of the state claim these new ones shall come from the south, and the south claim they should come from the north, and the taxpayers are so sore about having to hire extra ones that they don't care where they come from, but are telling 'em where to go." (April 3, 1931.)

Will says they have gone too far with this tax stuff.

"Wait a minute here now.

"It's all right for Jack Garner's reformed Congress –

"To pour it onto the rich with income taxes;

"To fine a man for dying;

"To put a tax on malt till they make it cost like beer, even if it don't taste like it;

"To refuse to pass a sales tax, then turn around and tax everything that is sold;

"To put a tax on matches and drive the U.S. to the insane asylum trying to make cigar lighters work —

"All these fool things come under the heading of Congressional employment.

"But, when they put a tax on chewing gum, the only thing left for a poor man to chew, that's going too far." (March 30, 1932.)

Are you getting your money's worth yet?

"The No. 2 president went down to Washington to confer with Huey Long and Herbert Hoover. With Hoover about firewood in the White House basement and Long on international and national affairs.

"Every U.S. citizen is taxed $77 a head. That's $10 more than last year. Every wage earner has been cut from 10 to 50 per cent, but the cost of being governed has taken a 12 ½ per cent raise.

"Then you hear birds say, 'All you need to restore prosperity is confidence.' Yeah? Well, you will help restore prosperity if you put taxes in proportion to the benefits you receive for them, the same as any other commodity. Did you receive $10 more protection this year than last?" (Jan. 20, 1933.)

"Congressman Green, chairman of the ways and means committee and in favor of strong inheritance taxes for the rich, has been made some kind of judge at an increased salary.

"It's funny the administration never thought of giving Borah or Jim Reed or Walsh some judeship where it would keep them from ferreting out so much Republican devilment. I'll bet all three of them could get appointments to the Supreme bench tomorrow if they would take it." (March 6, 1928.)

Chapter 15: War and Military

There must be another way

"Well, lots of war news in the papers today. I knew it was coming when I saw that we had cut down on our Army and Navy.

"If you want to know when a war is coming just watch the United States and see when they start cutting down on their defense. It's the surest barometer in the world.

"The Democrats have one great failing (that I was in hopes they had lived down) and that is they just want to fix the affairs of the world.

"Now it's big hearted and it's mighty generous, but it's just not possible for me (3,000 miles away) to tell you what caliber gun to have in your house. You know your neighbors better than I do." (May 16, 1933.)

You think Will was far off? Look at this:

"Looking beyond the wars he inherited, President Barack Obama on Thursday launched a reshaping and shrinking of the military. He vowed to preserve U.S. pre-eminence even as the Army and Marine Corps shed troops and the administration considers reducing its arsenal of nuclear weapons." -- Robert Burns of the Associated Press in St. Joseph News-Press, Jan. 6, 2012.

Oh, it's happened before (too many times).

"The Navy called in Admiral Magruder. He said the Navy was spending too much money.

"There is only one unpardonable thing you can say either in Navy, Army or politics, and that is to propose to cut down its expenditures. You can accuse them of negligence and even laziness, but to suggest spending less money! Well, he just lost his compass in mid-ocean." (Oct. 26, 1927.)

"There is one thing in common with all revolutions (in fact they are pretty near like wars in that respect) nobody ever knows what they are fighting about."

"The difference between a bandit and a patriot is a good press agent."

There are a lot of problems with wars, and one of those problems is paying for them.

"I been reading and studying over President Coolidge's message to Kansas and Missouri. He brought out Mr. Harding's idea (he didn't say it was, but it was) about the conscription of all wealth in case of war.

"That sounds fine after the war is over. Funny nobody thought of it before the last war started, and I doubt if you hear anything of it just before the start of the next one. If they did do it, it would be a great enlistment boost for war, and we all know thousands that would go themselves just to see some of the money taken away from the ones that copped it during the last war." (Nov. 13, 1926.)

And he added to this thought:

"Mr. Coolidge said in the next war we would draft wealth as well as men. Now everybody is arguing if it's practical. Why not postpone having the next war till the cause of it is so popular that you won't have to conscript either of them? If you will wait till we are invaded and everybody knows what they are fighting for, you won't need conscription." (Nov. 17, 1926.)

Will we ever stop having wars? (No.)

"A sure certainty about our Memorial days is as fast as the

ranks from one war thin out, the ranks from another take their place.

"Prominent men run out of Decoration Day speeches, but the world never runs out of wars. People talk peace, but men give their life's work to war. It won't stop till there is as much brains and scientific study put to aid peace as there is to promote war." (May 31, 1929.)

Oh, oh, here comes another one. (We are not involved yet.)

"I see where England has recognized the government of Russia. That means that war is practically assured with Russia and China, and they are getting all set for the old war contracts. They all learned something from us in the last one. Watch us start recognizing, too.

"You know there is nothing that makes a disreputable nation look respectable as quick as to have it give you a fat war contract. All our highly civilized nations are great humanitarians, but if two countries are going to kill each other off neutrals at least would like the privilege of furnishing the ammunition.

"When the judgment day comes, civilization will have an alibi: 'I never took a human life, I only sold the fellow the gun to take it with.'" (July 15, 1929.)

The war seems to get closer.

"The thing that makes me believe that China and Russia will fight is that nobody knows what they are fighting about.

"Newspapers are always offering prizes for the best definition of our Constitution, or 'how to solve prohibition,' and every other unknown subject. Why don't some of them offer a prize for a definition of what the last war started over? That would be the biggest bit of news of our generation.

"So it looks like this will be another typical war." (July 16, 1929.)

And even closer.

"Russia has called home her diplomats from China. China has called home hers from Russia. If they had both done that before the argument was started there would have been no argument.

"That's why diplomats don't mind starting a war, because it's a custom that they are to be brought safely home before the trouble starts. There should be a new rule saying: 'If you start a war while you are your country's official handicap to some other country, you have to stay with any war you start.'" (July 18, 1929.)

But wait! Maybe they are not so dumb after all.

"Mr. Ramsay MacDonald says that England got the worst of it in the late war. Say, Ramsay, if any man could figure out who got the worst of it out of the last war he could go down in history with Confucius and Calvin Coolidge.

"That's one good thing about wars. It takes smarter men to figure out who loses 'em than it does to start 'em. When China and Russia didn't start this late uprising that led me to believe that China, as ignorant as they are, and Russia, as dumb as they are, are the two most highly civilized nations on the face of the globe. The more ignorant you are the quicker you fight." (Aug. 11, 1929.)

Will comes up with a plan to end wars.

"I got a great scheme for universal peace, this United States of Europe that Briand is forming in Europe, with twenty nations in it, to be run like our forty-eight states are.

"Well, here is the scheme; have them adopt prohibition, and that will start 'em all arguing over it so much that it will get their minds off war. You can't fight, and argue prohibition. You are useless for anything else on earth.

"P.S. – And if this friendship of nations works over there, let's put Arizona and California in it. We can't get 'em to work with our bunch." (July 18, 1930.)

Good grief, here they go again! This time it's Japan.

"Papers say the Japanese are marching on Chinchow.

"Didn't I tell you last week they was going to take it about Xmas time? When these Japanese run a war they run it on schedule.

"That's not a bad Xmas present. This new part they are taking is as big as Oklahoma.

"This washes your League of Nations up. This slapped them right in the face." (Dec. 28, 1931.)

Wait a minute, something's changed.

"In one column of our morning papers the war had been called off, but they hadn't notified the other column.

"The Japanese say they don't want China, and it's a cinch the Chinese don't want Japan. The Japanese say if the Chinese would get back twenty miles from Shanghai that they would quit fighting. The Chinese say if the Japanese would go back home, where they belong, they would quit fighting.

"So nobody really knows what they are fighting over. It's almost like a civilized European war in that respect." (March 1, 1932.)

Wars between nations are bad enough, but then Will Rogers gets himself involved in a serious dispute.

"I was pretty worried last week. I am a Colonel on Alfalfa Bill Murray's Oklahoma 'fighting staff.' I thought he overmatched hisself. Take on Kansas till we get in practice, then Texas in the finals.

"When I heard 'Old Bill' hisself had hid a long squirrel rifle under his mustache and gone to the wars 'in person,' I said to myself, 'Col. Rogers, you better go into rehearsal.'

"So, I got myself a chemist and we started to work. The only way to lick a Texan is with bad liquor. Any state that can make worse liquor than Texas can lick 'em, but it's hard to make worse. That's why Texas licked Mexico. Texas had the worst. They fattened on Mexico's 'tequilla.' (July 28, 1931.)

That was just the warmup. Two years later things reached the boiling point.

"War Lord Bill Murray has called us Oklahomans to arms again.

"Most states use their National Guard for parading purposes, but Bill will call his out just like you ring for ice water.

"There is a river between Oklahoma and Texas. Bill owns half of it and Ma Ferguson owns half. If they want to build a bridge let 'em build to the middle and turn around and go back. If they want a dam, let 'em dam their half and let our half alone.

"So I guess the next time you hear of me I will be standing in water up to my ankles, right in the middle of Red River, with an old squirrel rifle aimed at that giant octopus Texas, and if Bill says shoot I will shoot.

"We will show 'em they can't monkey with our half of the river." (July 31, 1933.)

Meanwhile, Will watches a new effort for nations to agree to stop having wars. (Ha! Ha!)

"The Disarmament Conference in Geneva adjourns just at the only time when it was about to agree. Now they will go home and study on it and return with their usual propositions. France will want England to sink their navy. England will agree to France sinking their army. Both will want Germany to sink her remembrances, and all three agree on Italy sinking Mussolini.

"Asking Europe to disarm is like asking a man in Chicago to give up his life insurance. We can preach 'good-will,' but if we lived in Europe among those hyenas we would be in war before we got our grip unpacked. While we are having Washington Days and Lincoln Days, let's have a 'Thank the Atlantic Ocean Day.'" (May 8, 1929.)

Ah, but there is a little progress. (Ain't there?)

"See where they are forming in Europe a new organization called 'The United States of Europe.' Nobody knows just what it is or what its aims are, but we ought to be for it if only for one reason; and that is, it's the first thing been formed since the war that we haven't been asked to go over and join.

"If it's an economic boycott against our high Republican tariff I don't see why the Democrats wouldn't be allowed to join it.

"I guess this epidemic of forming clubs and things, that we have just so disastrously passed through, is just hitting Europe." (Sept. 12, 1929.)

They plod on and on.

"Well, the conference is synthetic now. They have decided to hold no public meetings (in London). The big one yesterday was just a decoy.

"Now they meet secretly and disarm synthetically. We won't really hear what was done at this conference till we read one of the delegates' memoirs after the next war. Writers are searching for fast boats home. They have some Marines here, so they can just tell it to the Marines and the Marines can tell it to us. If any American correspondent sends any news home today, he has made it up." (Jan. 22, 1930.)

For a change of pace, Will switches from troubles in Europe to South America.

"Other nations' troubles are not gloated over by us, but it does seem good to be able to read of the revolutions in Argentina, Peru and Brazil and not read where 'American Marines have landed and have the situation well in hand.'

"If Mr. Hoover does nothing else but keep our Army and Navy at home, we can forgive him for not giving us rain, lower taxes and an inflated stock market.

"Won't it be wonderful if we ever live to see the day when any country can have its own revolution, and even a private and congenial war with a neighboring nation, without uninvited guests?" (Sept. 8, 1930.)

Will takes time out from wars to remember George Washington.

"Here is what George Washington missed by not living to his 199th birthday.

"He would have seen our great political system of 'equal rights to all and privileges to none' working so smoothly that 7,000,000 are without a chance to earn their living.

"He would see 'em handing out rations in peacetime that would have reminded him of Valley Forge. In fact, we have reversed the old system. We all get fat in war times and thin during peace.

"I bet after seeing us he would sue us for calling him 'Father.'" (Feb. 22, 1931.)

And Will tries to interview a government official:

"Scene in box stall in Rogers home: Secretary of War Hurley eating Rogers's 'fodder':

"'Mr. Hurley, this is not for publication, but should the Philippines have their freedom?'

"'Will, this is a good administration, you see if it ain't.'

"'Now, Pat, you was in both China and Japan. Just what is their troubles?'

"'I'll tell you, Will, Hoover is a very warm, sympathetic man when you know him.'

"'Mr. Secretary, will that Russian plan work?'

"'Listen, Will, they haven't got a soul they can run against us.'

"So I just fed him and slept him for nothing. The next Cabinet officer pays his board." (Oct. 22, 1931.)

The threat of war in Europe just won't go away.

"Say, this man Roosevelt not only makes Congress roll over and play dead but, by golly, he made this tough guy Hitler promise to bring sticks out of the water. Is there no end to this man's cleverness?

"Course there is one thing about Europe. You can never believe 'em the first time. They will agree to anything till it come times to sign up.

"This might be just the ideal time to stop a war, for nobody has anything to fight one with. Like disarmament, it's not done for humanitarian reasons, it's only done for economic reasons.

"The whole thing seems too good to be true, but the whole world is changing, so maybe they are going to turn human." (May 17, 1933.)

Big surprise – things begin to get worse.

"Now Europe is saying that they didn't get so sore at what Mr. Roosevelt said as they did the way he said it. You see diplomats have a thing they call diplomatic language. It's just lots of words, and when they are all added up, they don't mean anything. Well, on account of the president having something to say, and wanting to say it, there is no diplomatic language for that. A diplomat has a hundred ways of saying nothing, but no way of saying something, because he has never had anything to say. That's why they call 'em diplomats.

"I have always said that a conference was held for one reason only, to give everybody a chance to get sore at everybody else. Sometimes it takes two or three conferences to scare up a war, but generally one will do it. I'll bet there was never a war between two nations that had never conferred first." (July 5, 1933.)

And things keep getting warmer.

"Austria? Say isn't that down there about in shooting distance of where the other war broke out?

"England has told Germany to 'lay off.' Now what if Germany don't 'choose' to lay off?

"The boys are looking around now, kinder choosing up sides again. Russia would like to look down that way. But she can't take her eyes off Japan long enough. Mussolini is waiting for the best offer. France has got every propeller a spinning.

"Now is one of the best times in the world for us to fight among ourselves. It will at least keep us out of some bigger devilment." (Feb. 14, 1934.)

Is there no stopping this? (No.)

"Been reading all the Sunday articles by world known writers and they all talk war.

"Well, if there is any excuse for anybody fighting at this time, it's beyond me. The consensus of opinion is that, 'so and so has to fight so and so sooner or later.' Well, I believe if I had to fight a man 'sooner or later' I would fight him later, and later the better.

"The only legitimate reason I can see why Germany and France must fight is they haven't fought in sixteen years, and the only reason I can see why us and Japan has to fight is because we haven't fought before." (March 25, 1934.)

(Nobody could slow down what was about to happen.)

Chapter 16: The World

"All the world's a stage. . ."

"Here we go again! America is running true to form, fixing some other country's business for 'em just as we always do. We mean well, but will wind up wrong as usual.

"When some nation wants us to help 'em they use the same old 'gag,' that we should exert our 'moral leadership' and, like a yap, believe it, when, as a matter of truth, no nation wants any other nation exerting a 'moral leadership' over 'em even if they had one.

"If we ever pass out as a great nation we ought to put on our tombstone, 'America died from a delusion that she had moral leadership.'" (June 22, 1931.)

Will can't figure out Russia.

"Me and my destitute friend Arthur Brisbane can't seem to get together on Russia.

"There is a thousand things I talk about that I don't know any more about than a senator, but I did take an airplane three years ago and flew from London to Moscow, and Leningrad, stayed there a couple of weeks, went with no delegation, and wasn't personally conducted. Saw everything, didn't even belong to a Hoover committee and I don't know any more about Russia than Brisbane does.

"If I wanted to start an insane asylum that would be 100 per cent cuckoo, I would just admit applicants that thought they knew something about Russia." (Sept. 14, 1930.)

But Brisbane has an answer.

"With all our interest attracted to Russian activities this week, I was joking Mr. Brisbane about me having been there and not him.

"Last night I got a cute letter from him which read:

"'Years ago European artists were kidding an American artist for painting scenes in Europe and yet he had never been over there. He replied, "Well, Leonardo de Vinci painted a pretty fair picture of the Lord's Supper and he didn't even have a ticket to it."

"He is serious about this Russia. He thinks they are going to get somewhere. Well, anyhow they got our Congress scared and that's more than our country has been able to do with 'em." (Sept. 25, 1930.)

But Will does know a little more about England.

"That England has one great custom in the government. They can bring before the House of Commons, in open session, any Cabinet member or the premier and ask him what he has done and what he has in mind for the future, and he has to tell 'em. Today they questioned Mr. MacDonald himself about the conference.

"We don't do it over here. It would be too embarrassing to our officials to have to admit what little they had done, and extremely humiliating to explain what they had in mind for the future when they had nothing in mind.

"After their appointment, if they are not impeached, we never hear of them again. They only have one obligation here. They have to sign the payroll in person." (Feb. 12, 1930.)

Even the king gets into the act, as Will attends a disarmament conference in London.

"These are happy times in England. The whole country is celebrating the victory of King George over Big Bill Thompson and Chicago.

"It is especially gratifying over here, for at one time things looked very bad for the king, as Big Bill had told him to keep his snoot out of Chicago affairs, which was a terrific blow to his majesty, as he had always taken such a personal interest and pride in Chicago. It was really one of his most cherished municipalities, and to find that they are still loyal to him even though out of funds pleases his royal highness beyond measure.

"Well, the conference met today and appointed a commission to meet tomorrow and appoint a delegation who will eventually appoint a committee to draw up ways and means of finding out what to start with first." (Jan. 28, 1930.)

A few earlier comments about that conference.

"Say, this sinking conference already is a success. The American delegation met this afternoon and went into conference at once at the American bar and sunk a fleet of schooners without warning.

"They brought eighteen young typewriters with 'em. That's four and a half blondes to the delegate, and I can write in long-hand left-handed, everything that will be done here in the next month.

"But say, the blondes cleaned up. Nobody looked at a delegate.

"They even brought some Marines on the boat to show it was a peace conference." (Jan. 17, 1930.)

Anybody for a revolution?

"We used to have a rule that our government wouldn't recognize any new government that had come into power by force and revolution. Then somebody that had accidentally read our history happened to ask,'Well, how did our government come into power?' So now we recognize 'em no matter who they shot to get in. Yesterday we took in Argentina, Bolivia and Peru. All you have to promise is that you will buy something from us, even if it's only guns for the next revolution.

"If Russia will just shave, and buy some tractors, we will recognize them. There is no such thing as a thief any more, as long as he can pay his way." (Sept. 19, 1930.)

"When the big nations quit meddling then the world will have peace."

"I don't care how little your country is, you got a right to run it like you want to."

But the U.S. doesn't often pay attention to that kind of advice.

"Now look out Democratic administration; you are about to revert to the old Republican type. You are telling some Latin American country who can be president and who can't.

"There is no doubt that Cuba is run 'cockeyed,' but what country ain't?

"Now, we get our sugar from Cuba, and anything we do in Cuba is going to be misunderstood.

"So about the best thing we can do in Cuba is to let Cuba take care of Cuba." (Aug. 9, 1933.)

Will enjoyed traveling around the United States, especially by those new-fangled airplanes, and he also liked to visit foreign nations. One of his favorite stops was England.

"England's House of Parliament, or Commons rather (I have seen it and prefer calling it the Commons), closed today to give some of the lady members a chance to try and swim the English Channel.

"I wanted to have my wife try it, but the Channel is all booked up for the next week." (Aug. 4, 1926.)

"The League of Nations to perpetuate peace is in session. On account of Spain not being in the last war, they won't let her in.

If you want to help make peace, you have to fight for it." (Sept. 3, 1926.)

"Parliament, which had adjourned, has just today called a special session within a few days. If we ever did a thing like that in the summer we would have to hold it in Europe or out on a Chautauqua circuit, so we could get a few members present.

"Queer people, these English legislators. They are satisfied to stay in their own country; in fact, they rather like it." (Aug. 24, 1926.)

He also liked places closer to home.

"Talk about 'having to see Paris' and 'so this is London' and 'must visit Claremore,' but till you have seen Agua Caliente, Mexico, you have just grown up ignorance. A beautiful spot, and the most sober and orderly crowd. Why, you wouldn't hardly believe they were Americans.

"Every nation must have its form of legalized gambling. We have our Wall Street. Mexico gives you a more even break. They have 'roulette,' a percentage of your losings go to the government. They are a primitive race. They put government above broker.

"Folks will take a chance. Old Noah gambled on not getting the 'foot and mouth' disease in there with all those animals, and old King Solomon bet a hundred women he wouldn't pay 'em alimony and won his bet. 'Viva la Mexico.'" (March 16, 1930.)

Sometimes he went by steamship (this telegram from the Steamship Ile de France):

"Rain spoiled it Sunday. H.L. Mencken and I were going to Hyde Park, London, where, if you have anything against the government or king, or even as low down as a sir, why jump up on a box and get it out of your system.

"They sink the navy, impeach the Crown and cancel the debts, and when they finish they are just as happy as if it had been done.

It's real democracy. Over home you have to be elected to the Senate before you can do it.

"I was going to enter Mencken. He says the system is still in vogue in Maryland, the only civilized state left." (Feb. 3, 1930.)

Aboard another steamship (S.S. Empress of Russia), Will crossed the international dateline.

"You know I told you we was going to lose a day for no other reason than to make somebody's calendar come out even. Well, we lost a day. We gained a typhoon. We lost a lifeboat and I lost my whole internal possessions. An old Oklahoma prairie product has no business on this ocean when it's washing away lifeboats. Brother, you got quite a spring freshet.

"Gibbons was broken hearted when we got through alive, for it spoiled a good story for him.

"I already found out enough on this trip to warrant coming, and this is if America will stay home and take care of our own business we need never fear Japan if she has to cross this ocean to get to us. If we can't lick a seasick soldier then we deserve to lose." (Nov. 27, 1931.)

Another steamship was the S.S. President Taft.

"Shanghai was a knockout. It's Brooklyn gone English. Say, where did they get this Chinese chop-suey stuff? I have run the legs off every rickshaw motorman in China, and nobody ever any more heard of it than Nevada did of Volstead.

"Another hoax was that a Chinaman's word was as good as his bond. Well, that goes with the chop suey. That might have been in the old days, but not since the missionaries and business men come in. Chinese are just as human and anybody now." (Jan. 1, 1932.)

And then he takes a look at the Middle East and Egypt.

"Today saw Jerusalem, Dead Sea and Bethlehem. Never catch

me traveling over here again unless I have read the Book. First, these Pyramids. Mexico's got bigger. And the Sphinx, Coolidge has got him licked to death.

"Tomorrow 600 miles of flying in a land plane to Athens; see if the Greeks got a word for that." (Jan. 15, 1932.)

"There's one thing no nation can ever accuse us of and that is secret diplomacy. Our foreign dealings are an open book. Generally a check book."

"They say all nations are sore at us, but unfortunately for us they didn't get sore at us quick enough. If they had, we would have saved money. We are the ones that should be sore at them for not getting sore quicker." (Dec. 29, 1926.)

Sometimes Will noticed an act of nature.

"See where America and Mexico had a joint earthquake. That's the only thing I ever heard that we split 50-50 with Mexico.

"Lucky for Mexico that she didn't grab off more of the earthquake than we did or she would have got a note from Kellogg.

"It's the influence from Moscow that is causing all this earth's upheaval." (Jan. 2, 1927.)

Will checks up on the Navy.

"Had a visit today at the home of ex-Secretary of the Navy Josephus Daniels. He had all the photographs of our Navy, when we had a Navy.

"Wars don't diminish our Navy. It's peace that is so devastating, even our lifeboats shot from under us.

"Other nations were anxious to confer when we were building ahead of them, but now they are ahead, so why should they confer?

"P.S. – Congress ought to pass a law prohibiting us conferring with anybody on anything, till we learn how." (Feb. 1, 1927.)

The United States has had troops in Afghanistan for years, and they are still there in 2012. There is widespread demand to bring our troops home. There was some trouble in Afghanistan in Will Rogers's day, too.

"Well, they finally stopped us from sending Marines to every war we could hear of. They are having one in Afghanistan. The thing will be over before Congress can pronounce it, much less find out where it is located.

"It seems the king over there thought he was adopting modern ideas by limiting his subjects to one wife per each. No wonder they threw him out. He was just old-fashioned and didn't know it. He wasn't modern. He was just queer." (Dec. 19, 1928.)

Will wonders about the World Court.

"This World Court is up again. Some think it's great and some think it's terrible, and I am just one of 90 per cent of our population who don't know what it is. The more I read about both sides the less I know about the middle.

"Each nation that goes into it has it understood, with a reservation, that anything the court does shall be binding, except in cases pertaining to them. But everybody is agreed on one thing and that is if we ratify it, it would be a crowing achievement to finish out the great career of Mr. Elihu Root, a great man and splendid statesman.

"Others think we could pay him our obligation in a cheaper way." (Sept. 6, 1929.)

The news from England does not surprise Will.

"Well, America was finally notified 'diplomatically' that England wouldn't pay the debt.

"That's what practically all the people in both nations knew all the time, but even though a diplomat is the last person to find anything out, I knew the news would finally leak out to 'em.

"The news hit us like the news that Babe Ruth bats left-handed.

"But was we downhearted? No, sir. On that very day Congress voted seven billions. So our own credit is all right.

"From now on we will do all our borrowing and loaning on the home grounds." (June 5, 1934.)

They have diplomats in China, too. In this telegram from Providence, R.I., Will remembers chop suey.

"When American diplomacy gets through messing us around over in China, I can tell them what has caused this hate of us over there. It's our missionaries who have been trying to introduce 'chop suey' into China. China didn't mind them eating it there, but when they tried to call it a Chinese dish that's what made them start shooting at us.

"P.S. – This is Rhode Island, the place where half their legislature went out of the state and hid one time, and the state never run better in its life than it did then." (May 15, 1927.)

Once more Will takes a hard look at diplomats.

"All we seem to celebrate Washington's for is so we can revive the argument as to 'what he had to say about entanglements with Europe.' Every speaker makes him say just what that speaker wants him to say. Coolidge says it was Jefferson that made the 'wise crack' about not messing with outsiders.

"So it looks like added to all his other accomplishments Washington was a diplomat. A diplomat is one that says something that is equally misunderstood by both sides, and never clear to either." (Feb. 24, 1929.)

Speaking of diplomacy, here is the lack of same.

"So Mayor Walker stood Mahatma Gandhi up and went to a night club instead. As our Southern mothers always said, 'Raising will tell.'

"Gandhi, on viewing Buckingham Palace all illuminated, said: 'What an extravagance for a country trying to balance its budget!'" (Sept. 16, 1931.)

Will observes that you can't keep the Germans down.

"The German Zeppelin is on its round-the-world trip. The German steamship Bremen broke the world's record in crossing the Atlantic. Their commerce is getting back strong. All of these things are the greatest illustration that war is useless.

"They were getting too strong commercially for some other nations fifteen years ago, now the war has been over eleven years and they are excelling in the same things again. It don't do no good to whip a man if he is beating you at anything. When he gets up he can still beat you at the same things. You only delay him, you don't stop him." (Aug. 14, 1929.)

And then there is Mussolini of Italy.

""Mussolini woke up yesterday, felt tired and worn so he gave up seven of his Cabinet positions. I wouldn't be surprised to see him become so indolent that he took up golf. All he is now is manager of Italy and supervisor of the seven positions that he gave up.

"And over here we take one Cabinet job serious. Even the South got sore because Mr. Hoover didn't appoint one of them on his Cabinet. He was mighty honest about it, though. He said there is lots of men down there big enough but they are not smart enough to be Republicans." (Sept. 13, 1929.)

Will feels sorry for the League of Nations.

"Every morning some nation issues Japan an ultimatum to quit fighting China, and every time she gets another ultimatum she sends in another army.

"Poor League of Nations! They have written Japan so much

they have run out of stationery. She don't even open their notes any more.

"That League was a great thing to make the little fellow behave, but when the big fellows want to get away with anything it has no more power than a Senate investigating committee." (Oct. 13, 1931.)

Chapter 17: This and That

All this stuff must fit in somewhere. . .

"Celebrating 'Mother's Day' by giving 'Ma' Rogers a vacation. Picked her a white desert flower and walked her for seven miles through the celebrated Carlsbad Caverns.

"I thought the biggest hole in the ground was when you were drilling for oil and struck a dry hole, but this is bigger than even that. It's just the Grand Canyon with a roof over it.

"Then, when you get inside, it's got all the cathedrals of the world in it, with half of 'em hanging upside down.

"If a 'drunk' suddenly woke up in that great hall in there, he would think he had died and gone to heaven, for that's the nearest thing to his imagination of the place." (May 10, 1931.)

Will has a thought about big game hunting.

"Been looking at the pictures in the papers today of some woman that killed at lot of big game in India.

"I wish the Humane Society would take up one thing – after killing a poor dumb animal, you are not allowed to sit on it or have your picture made. That's awful humiliating to a wild animal. I believe they got the same old stuffed lion and elephant and tiger over there that they all have their pictures taken on." (June 15, 1930.)

A few stray thoughts:

"History ain't what it is. It's what some writer wanted it to be."

"You would be surprised what there is to see in this great country within 200 miles of where any of us live. I don't care what state or what town."

"Trouble with American transportation is that you can get somewhere quicker than you can think of a reason for going there. What we need now is a new excuse to go somewhere."

"Everybody likes to hear it straight from the boss, even if you are going to get fired."

"If you want to ship off fat beef cattle at the end of their existence, you have got to have 'em satisfied on the range."

"I hope we never see the day when a thing is as bad as some of our newspapers make it."

Flooding in the Southern states prompts Will to call for aid.

"I hate to keep digging on it, but we still have 600,000 of our own whose homes are now floating toward Nicaragua. We can't seem to get the government interested in them financially.

"I wish you would send some checks to the Red Cross in New Orleans. I am going there next Wednesday night, June 1, to give a benefit, and it already has more money assured than any one given in any part of the country. Why? Because they are right there and they know the needs of the people.

"If 600,000 people had lost their all and were being fed by charity in the East they would raise fifty millions in a day. Come on, let's help them, even if they are not Americans. They can't help it because of their nationality." (May 27, 1927.)

Will ponders scientist Albert Einstein.

"Einstein left New York flat and is headed for Hollywood.

"If he's got a theory that nobody knows what it is, or what it's all about, why there is a half dozen companies here that will buy it and produce it along with these enigmas of our own that we put out.

"His theory is that 'there is no space.' Wait till he sees the vacant room on some of these miniature golf courses.

"Well, we will be waiting for him here. Hollywood can meet him on equal terms. We don't know what his 'racket' is, or vice versa." (Dec. 15, 1930.)

Meanwhile, Will tries his luck again on steamships.

Aboard the S.S. Bremen: "My remaining days are dedicated to annihilate the slogan 'Big Boats Don't Rock.' Say, the higher they are the further they rock. They tail spin, slip slide, and ground loop. It's taken a good man to stay tied in bed today. Well, here's how bad it is: There is not an American in the bar-room, and when I think of those poor senators on the George Washington, may the Almighty have pity on a poor peace delegation on a dry boat out on a night like this.

"The more I see of steamship travel the less I think of the hardship of Lindbergh. If I can find a pilot that wants to fly to America, I will be his Levine, and this goes as an advertisement." (Jan. 13, 1930.)

Changing ships doesn't help.

Aboard the S.S. Ile de France: "I have nothing to say and feel in no shape to say it in if I did have. Lindbergh's ocean is as sore at the world as a defeated candidate.

"When I hinted that I would fly back if I could, I received a lot of cables offering to take me on, among them Mrs. Keith Miller, one of our best airshees. My wife is not jealous, but she just never did like to have me stay out over the ocean all night with a strange woman or even a friendly woman. If we could have got in before dark she wouldn't have minded. Course we could have taken a chaperon but not as much gas, but gas is more beneficial on a trip like that than a chaperon. It was just unfortunate all round." (Feb. 2, 1930.)

Aboard the S.S. Empress of Russia: "When you reach the 180th meridian west you lost a whole day. Don't ask me why. It's all Wickersham to me.

"If you come back this way you get it back. If you don't you just lose it. The way days are now it don't look like it's worth coming back for.

"We go to bed tomorrow night, Thursday, and wake up Saturday, maybe. We come pretty near losing Thursday, Thanksgiving. Guess lots of folks wish they could skip this Thanksgiving. Getting less cause for it every year. It's just about a bust with everybody that don't raise turkeys or cranberries to sell." (Nov. 25, 1931.)

A few more stray thoughts by Will, this time about religion and sort of philosophy:

"What constitutes a life well spent, anyway? Love and admiration from your fellow men is all that any one can ask."

"Some people spend a lifetime juggling with words, with not an idea in a carload."

"I was raised predominantly a Methodist but I have traveled so much, mixed with so many people in all parts of the world, I don't know just now what I am. I know I have never been a non-believer. But I can honestly tell you that I don't think that any one religion is the religion."

"I bet any Sunday could be made as popular at church as Easter is if you made 'em fashion shows too. The audience is so busy looking at each other that the preacher just as well recite Gunga Dun."

"If they are going to argue religion in the church instead of teaching it, no wonder you see more people at a circus than at a church."

"Statistics have proven there are twenty five bath tubs sold to every Bible."

"Whoever wrote the Ten Commandments made 'em short. They may not always be kept but they can be understood."

Will investigates worm ranches.

"California always did have one custom that they took serious, but it amused the rest of the United States. That was in calling everything a 'ranch.' Everything big enough to spread a double mattress on is called a 'ranch.'

"Well, up here in these mountains where there is lots of fishing, why every house you pass they sell fishing worms, and it's called a 'worm ranch.'

"Well, I always did want to own a ranch, so I am in the market for a good worm ranch. I never was so hot as a cowboy, but I believe I would make a good 'worm herder.'

"If I can land our presidents as clients, I could make it sound like England when they sell to the king, 'Rogers's Worm Ranch, Purveyor to His Excellency, the President.'" (Aug. 30, 1932.)

"I bought my worm ranch. The man is to turn over two thousand yearling worms, two thousand two-year-olds, five hundred bull worms and the rest is a mixed breed.   "Now, I find in these Sierra Nevadas they are fishing with grasshoppers, so got a grasshopper ranch adjoining. Am going to do a little Luther Burbank, cross my grasshoppers and worms and produce an animal that if the fish don't bite at him, he will bite the fish, so you get your fish anyhow.

"I am no fisherman and hope I never get lazy enough to take it up. I am in these mountains on an essential industry (ask Bill Hayes), but these loafers up here tell me that the fish are not biting this year, and you would be surprised the votes Hoover is losing." (Sept. 4, 1932.)

Will wonders about jurors.

"Our attention in the last few days has been focused on juries, and from what we read about it the personal opinion of the jurymen after listening to all the testimony don't seem to mean much.

"It's how strong-minded and persuasive some other jurymen are. Look at the fall case, first ballot, seven for acquittal, two undecided, and only three for conviction, yet in the end the three switched all the others.

"It wasn't the evidence, for they had heard it all before they took the first ballot. So it looks like a lot of jurymen ought to be lawyers, for they are evidently more convincing than the lawyers." (Oct. 28, 1929.)

Then he switches to cosmetics.

"As there was more money spent on cold cream and cosmetics last year than on bacon and beans, why naturally there must be more people interested in beautifying themselves.

"The international beauty congress met in New York yesterday and they figured out that this rubbing something on your head to prevent baldness is really what causes it. They claim that you got to take stuff internally for it.

"So from now on if you see a bald-headed bird reach for his flask, don't ask him for a swig. It's only irrigation juice for his roof." (March 12, 1931.)

A few more pearls of wisdom:

"The time ain't far off when a woman won't know any more than a man."

"When newspapers knock a man a lot, there is sure to be a lot of good in him."

"Make every speaker as soon as he tells all he knows, sit down.

That will shorten our speeches so much you will be out by lunch time."

"We should never reach so high that we would ever forget those who helped us get there."

Will talks about parades.

"This is 'fiesta' day in Santa Barbara (California). The other days in Santa Barbara are 'siesta' days. (If you don't speak all these languages it's not my fault.)

"Hundreds and hundreds of beautiful horses in the parade, and a man without a silver-mounted saddle up here is a vagrant. Everybody in Spanish costumes. These big blond Iowans look kinder funny in 'em but they have 'em on (sometimes backwards).

"Every town should have some kind of yearly celebration. (I am writing like Brisbane.) Didn't Rome have its annual bathing festival? Didn't Cairo have some kind of female rodeo? Albany, N.Y., is going to make the Walker investigation a yearly fall festival.

"So think up something for your town to celebrate. Have a parade. Americans like to parade. We are a parading nation. 'Upluripus paraditorius (some paraders).'" (Aug. 18, 1932.)

Looking into the future a bit.

"Back to the old home state (Oklahoma). The governor had just made me Colonel on his staff and I come home to put out a mint bed.

"The state never looked better and politics never looked worse, which is as it should be. Just missed by one day a reunion of the writers of our state Constitution, which was celebrating its twenty-second birthday, and beautiful tribute was paid there to my father, who was the oldest member of the Constitution founders.

"If Oklahoma does in the next twenty-two years what we have in the last, why New York will be our parking space, Chicago our arsenal, New Orleans our amusement centre and Los Angeles segregated for Elk and Shrine conventions." (Sept. 18, 1929.)

Debating disarmament.

"Went down last night to hear an Oklahoma University debating team against California, 'To disarm, or not disarm.' Our first debating team is over in London, on the same subject and with the same results, only this team goes home when the debate is over.

"These have debated all over the country on this subject, on both sides of the argument, and they told me a very surprising thing. The side against 'disarmament' always wins. They explained the fact because disarmament was a theory and an ideal and that the other side could shoot our argument full of holes." (March 19, 1930.)

Will has decided where he will retire.

"The old desert; the more you see of it the more you can understand folks really loving it.

"It's a great health giver to many a disabled soul. It's just like a lot of folks. It never had a chance. The minute you give it any water it grows more stuff than all your fertile land.

"These old boys sitting away out here don't look like they have to worry whether Mr. Hoover's letter to the drys will keep them in line... Their living has got to come from a well and a pump and not from any political patronage, so these fellows escape all that political 'hooey' that hits us every four years.

"Yes, sir, when we retire from active life, it's the Senate or the desert, and by golly I believe I will go to the desert." (Aug. 24, 1932.)

One moment Will likes parades, and the next he is not so sure.

"Well, today was St. Patrick's Day. But do you think they would parade on Sunday? No, sir. There wouldn't be any traffic to block if you used Fifth Avenue on Sunday.

"You know there is nothing as overestimated as a parade of any kind. It don't draw crowds, the people that are lined along the sidewalk are just trying to get to the other side. That's all. Nobody is interested in a parade but the fellow marching and his family who are compelled to go see how bad he marches. Every city should have one street away out where it won't interfere with business or traffic, call it Parade Street, then let any organization go there and march till they dropped. Do that and see how big an audience they can draw." (March 17, 1929.)

Moving right along to furniture.

"If it ain't one calamity hits us it's another.

"Did you read where Jesse Livermore, E.F. Hutton, Marshall Field, Frelinghuysen, Sloan of General Motors and Ferrell of U.S. Steel, and a host of others, have been buying their 'antique' furniture in England before it was even aged in the wood. They couldn't make these new antique 'high boys' fast enough for our rich 'old boys.'

"This expose will bring a hardship on our wealthy. It's liable to force 'em to use American made furniture. Us middle class over here never have to worry having old furniture to point out to our friends. We buy it on payments and before it's paid for it's plenty antique." (Oct. 9, 1930.)

It's graduation time.

"My daughter graduated yesterday at a girls' preparatory school. They read off course each girl had taken. When they said, 'Mary Rogers, diploma in English' I had to laugh at that. One of my children studying English – why, it's just inherited. You don't have to study it in our family.

"Doug Fairbanks had a niece graduating, Wallace Beery had a relation, Frank Lloyd, the great director, a daughter, and all four of us just sat there and purred like four old tomcats basking in a little reflected sunshine and secretly congratulating ourselves on choosing a profession where education played no part." (June 12, 1931.)

There's something about that English Channel...

"Another American woman just now swam in from France. Her husband was carried from the boat suffering from cold and exposure. She has two children, the smallest a girl, who is swimming over tomorrow.

"Yours for a revised edition of the dictionary explaining which is the weaker sex." (Aug. 28, 1926.)

"I imagine it's been said before, and I don't claim this as an entirely new observation, but radio is a great thing. I believe it's our greatest invention, far greater than the automobile, for it don't kill anybody. It don't cost us millions in roads. When we are too lazy, or too old to do anything else, we can listen in." (Feb. 23, 1930.)

"Just come from England, Ark., the town you read about, where the people wanted food. It seemed mighty peaceful and happy now. Went to the school there, where the children were being fed at lunch time all they wanted of fine vegetable soup, cooked in a big vat, that had been a whiskey still and presented to the cause by a patriotic moonshiner.

"This is the very heart of the most needy section in America. And yet it's the most fertile land you ever saw. But the country people absolutely have nothing.

"The Red Cross as usual are doing great work. In just these

two counties I visited today they are feeding 8,000 families, with an average of six to the family. You don't know what hard times are till you go into some of these houses. The weather is with 'em now, but if it turns cold there will be a lot of suffering.

"This is not a plea, it's just a report, but it's the worst need I ever saw." (Jan. 23, 1931.)

# # #

Special Thanks

As noted in the Acknowledgement at the front of this book, the author would like to extend special thanks to the excellent staff personnel of the Will Rogers Memorial Museums in Claremore and Oologah, Okla. They provided invaluable resources including the Telegrams written by Will Rogers, parts of which are quoted throughout this book.

In particular, Steve Gragert tirelessly checked comments and quotes from Will Rogers to assure as much accuracy as possible. Thanks, Steve.

The author also would like to acknowledge two other sources, which were reviewed by the author. They include:

Will Rogers, written by Betty Rogers, wife of Will Rogers, published by the University of Oklahoma Press, Norman, 1941.

Will Rogers, Ambassador of Good Will and Prince of Wit and Wisdom, written by P.J. O'Brien, copyright 1935 in Great Britain and printed in the U.S.A.